HOME GIRLS

ALVINA E. QUINTANA

HOME GIRLS

Chicana
Literary Voices

TEMPLE UNIVERSITY PRESS

PHILADELPHIA

Temple University Press, Philadelphia 19122
Copyright © 1996 by Temple University
Published 1996
Printed in the United States of America

⊗ The paper used in this book meets the requirements of the American
National Standard for Information Sciences — Permanence of Paper for
Printed Library Materials, ANSI Z39.48–1984

Text design by Kate Nichols

Library of Congress Cataloging-in-Publication Data
Quintana, Alvina E., 1947–
    Home girls : Chicana literary voices / Alvina E. Quintana.
        p.   cm.
    Includes bibliographical references and index.
    ISBN 1–56639–372–8 (cloth : alk. paper). —
ISBN 1–56639–373–6 (paper : alk. paper)
        1. American literature — Mexican American authors — History and
criticism.   2. Women and literature — United States — History — 20th
century.   3. American literature — Women authors — History and
criticism.   4. Mexican American women — Intellectual life.
5. Mexican American women in literature.   6. Mexican Americans in
literature.   I. Title.
PS153.M4Q56   1996
810.9'9287'896872 — dc20   95–39751

For my parents,
Roberto Martinez Quintana (1900–1978)
and
Albina Carrasco Quintana

Contents

Contents

Acknowledgments

*H*ome Girls, a universal trope for women of color in the United States, has special significance for me because it conjures up a plethora of personal and cultural concerns. I am a native of San Francisco, California, now living in Newark, Delaware—a Chicana who thrives on the writing produced by my Chicana "Home Girls." For many people "home" summons notions of family and sanctuary—a space that nurtures and inspires growth. The Chicanas represented in this book develop conventional perceptions of "home" by enhancing our understanding of domestic, geographic, cultural, and discursive spaces, augmenting our awareness of the relationship between the Mexican Diaspora and the politics of Chicana writing.

Because many people made this book possible, I cannot imagine beginning without first acknowledging them. The project itself has taken many forms; first conceptualized as a scholarly activity, it gradually transformed into a spiritual contemplation concerning the notion of *home/culture*. The interdisciplinary impulse of this project was inspired by the intensely intellectual and supportive History of Consciousness Board of Studies at the University of California at Santa Cruz. I am particularly grateful for the scholarly encouragement and support of Hayden White, Marta Morello-Frosch, Josè Saldívar, James Clifford, Donna Haraway, Bettina Aptheker, Angela Davis, Fredric Jameson, and Susan Willis. Other members of the University of California at Santa Cruz community were also extremely supportive.

I am indebted to Sucheng Chan, May Diaz, Elba Sanchez, Katia Panas, Rosie Cabrera, Michael Grigsby, and Pedro Castillo, who assisted in keeping me emotionally and physically on track during my tenure at Santa Cruz. Ongoing discussions with my colleagues in graduate school — Katie King, Deborah Gordon, Ruth Frankenberg, Lata Mani, Elliott Butler Evans, Sandra Azevedo, Chela Sandoval, Caren Kaplan, Zoe Sofoulis, and Noel Sturgeon — also contributed to the production of this book. In addition, I cannot overlook the Chicana network at the University of California at Santa Barbara and my friendship and continuing critical conversations with Rosa Linda Fregoso and Sara Garcia.

In 1990 I received a post-doctoral fellowship from the University of California that provided financial support and afforded me the opportunity to further my studies in the Ethnic Studies Department at the University of California at Berkeley. I owe special thanks to "Las Furibundistas" Norma Alarcón, Elaine Kim, Marilyn Alquizola, Caridad Souza, Shelly Wong, and Guila Fabi for providing me with insights into comparative ethnic research and the intersections between feminism and nationalism.

My colleagues in the English Department at the University of

Acknowledgments

Delaware were also helpful during the time I was completing this project. Barbara Gates and Bonnie Scott have sustained and inspired me in countless ways since my arrival in Delaware. Mary Richards went beyond her responsibilities as the Dean of Arts and Science with her mentoring and unfailing support during the final stages of this project. Special thanks to Ann Ardis, who took time out from her busy Administrator-Mother-Scholar schedule to read and comment on more than one version of this manuscript, and to Carol Henderson for helping me with the crucial but tedious proofreading phase of this work. Janet Francendese, editor and kindred spirit, kept me sane by guiding me through the entire book process with her sound judgment and wonderful sense of humor. I also benefited greatly from Bobbe Needham's exceptional editorial assistance.

This book would not have been possible without the love and encouragement of my family: my sisters Rosa Quintana and Carmen Guerrero, whose faith and loyalty inspired me to persevere; my daughters Sascha and Nanú, who absolved me of motherly guilt by being gracious and understanding when I spent hours away from them reading and writing; and my niece Linda Quintana-Duran, who enlightened me about ritual, metaphysics, and art, and contributed the cover art for this book. Edward and Eva Guerrero, understanding my need for solitude, not only supported my retreat in Mendocino County but provided the beautiful painting of the "North Coast wave" that helped center my energy in my home away from home. Finally, I want to thank my soul mate Edward Guerrero, who has lived with and talked me through all the issues raised in this book.

The following publishers have given permission to reprint poems contained herein:

Acknowledgments

"Legal Alien" by Pat Mora, p. 1, is reprinted with permission from the publisher of *Chants*. Houston: Arte Público Press–University of Houston, 1994, p. 52.

"Refugee Ship" by Lorna Dee Cervantes, p. 40, is reprinted with permission from the publisher of the *Revista Chicano-Riquena*. Houston: Arte Público Press–University of Houston, 1982.

Excerpt from "Marina Virgin," p. 41, is reprinted here by permission from Lucha Corpi, the poet, and Catherine Rodríguez-Nieto, the translator. It was first published in *Fireflight: Three Latin American Poets*. Berkeley: Oyez, 1976, p. 79.

"You Cramp My Style, Baby" by Lorna Dee Cervantes, p. 42, is reprinted with permission from the author. It first appeared in *Chisme Arte*.

Excerpts from "It's the Poverty" by Cherríe Moraga, pp. 49, 118–119, are reprinted with permission from the author. The poem is from *Loving in the War Years*: Lo Que Nunca Paso por Sus Labios. Boston: South End Press, 1983, p. 62–63.

Excerpts from "Mi Reflejo" by Lydia Camarillo, pp. 52, 53, are reprinted with permission from *La Palabra*, Vol. 2, no. 2 (Autumn), 1980, p. 73.

"To Live in the Borderlands Means You," pp. 140–142, from *Borderlands/La Frontera: The New Mestiza* © 1987 by Gloria Anzaldúa. Reprinted with permission from Aunt Lute Books (San Francisco, pp. 194–195).

HOME GIRLS

Introduction:
Testimonio as Biotheory

Legal Alien

Bi-lingual, Bi-cultural,
Able to slip from "How's life?"
to "Me 'stan volviendo loca,"
able to sit in a paneled office
drafting memos in smooth English,
able to order in fluent Spanish
at a Mexican restaurant,
American but hyphenated,
viewed by Anglos as perhaps exotic,
perhaps inferior, definitely different,
viewed by Mexicans as alien,
(their eyes say, "You may speak
Spanish but you're not like me")
an American to Mexicans
a Mexican to Americans
a handy token
sliding back and forth
between the fringes of both worlds
by smiling
by masking the discomfort
of being pre-judged
Bi-laterally.[1]

A s far back as I can remember, the two words *bilingual* and *bicultural* have acted as a kind of background rhythm to my existence. *Bilingual, bicultural* — terms that, as Pat Mora's "Legal Alien" illustrates, hyphenate experiences, creating at a minimum the doubling effect a number of writers have discussed, "an American to Mexicans, a Mexican to Americans." Because this doubling, this "polyphony" set by language and culture, is tantamount to the so-called minority American experience, it seems ironic that for some people the positioning between two cultures automatically equates with an "essentialized" minority perspective. Imagine throwing a pair of dice and always expecting them to fall in the same combination. This ludicrous expectation resembles the problematic reasoning that occurs whenever we speak of a universal minority experience. As a Chicana, I can testify that, more than the broad Mexican and American contexts, I trace my influences to the specific region in which I grew up and the geographic regions in which my parents were reared.

Two anecdotes illuminate some of the events that have motivated and inspired my research and contextualize my interest in identity politics. In the first story I am a kindergartner, in the second a graduate student.

My parents raised all nine of their children to respect their elders, to speak when spoken to, to go to church on Sundays, and generally to behave, which meant do not make any waves and stay out of trouble. We never thought of ourselves as bilingual or bicultural, even though we spoke Spanish and English at home. Although the staples of our diet were beans, rice, and tortillas, as a child I don't recall thinking that our meals were Mexican; we simply referred to them as breakfast, lunch, or dinner. In retrospect I have come to realize how my formal education, my induction into the world outside my family, transformed my assumptions in a way that made me keenly aware of my racialized status in America.

I went to kindergarten in an elementary school in San Francisco's Mission District. Today the Mission is thought of as a Latino community, but it was not always so. In the 1950s Irish Americans constituted the dominant ethnic population, a fact that became uncomfortably apparent to me during my first days in public school. Until I was about six, my major cultural influences had been my "Mexican" mother and father.

Meditating on my first days in Bryant School, I vividly recall what we now label, perhaps too familiarly, "difference." In her efforts to keep me well groomed and save precious time, my mother was in the habit of French braiding my hair. Every morning just before I left for school, she would part my hair down the middle and form two long braids, weaving colorful ribbons into them and folding each braid in a lasso loop that she fastened in place with a large bow just above each ear. I liked this hairdo; it accentuated the lovely gold-and-ruby dangling earrings my father had brought me from one of his annual pilgrimages to visit "his family" in Mexico. I was short and thin — smaller than most of my classmates — with a fair complexion, dark eyes, and dark brown hair that, unbraided, hung past my waist. My dresses were different in style and usually much more colorful than the subdued pastels of my classmates. (Since there were nine of us my mother saved money by making most of our clothes.)

Still, it wasn't the hair, the earrings, or the dresses that made me feel different; rather it was the question my classmates asked repeatedly during those first weeks: "What are you?" The first time I suppose I was a little thrown, but when child after child asked me to define myself, I began to feel increasingly uncomfortable.

Uneasy and uncertain about the appropriate response, I decided that I would take the challenge home to my parents for their consideration.

My home, unlike the one Richard Rodriguez describes in *Hunger of Memory,* was a private space in which we spoke Spanish as well as English. My mother, a native of Carizozo, New Mexico, always spoke to us children in English and to my father in Spanish; my father, born in Mexico City, refused to speak English at home though he was quite capable of it. The shape of this bilingual, bicultural environment my parents created also seemed to divide our home along gender lines. Early on I realized that in our home my mother functioned as the ultimate authority; as a homemaker, she was responsible for all the internal workings of our day-to-day existence. My father, a teamster warehouseman by trade, earned his living on the outside, spending much of his weekend time off working either as "El Vocero del Aire," a volunteer disc jockey on the local Mexican radio station, or performing administrative duties as president of el Comité Cívico Mexicano. He was the epitome of a public individual and served as the family mediator between our public and private worlds.

I vividly remember walking home from kindergarten that day, thinking that to understand the puzzling question "What are you?" I would need to explain in both English and Spanish, for I needed help from both my parents. That evening I headed for the kitchen where my mother busied herself with dinner preparations and told her about the question many of my classmates had been asking. She seemed intuitively aware of my confusion and gave me my answer without a moment's hesitation: "You are Spanish!"

When my father came home from work he always went straight to the large green recliner in front of the television set in our living room. Elevating his legs in a laid-back position, he relaxed by taking in the day's news as he waited for dinner to be served. In this quiet time animated only by the black-and-white images of the world that our television beamed in, I brought my concern to him. "Los niños en la escuela me han hecho una pregunta que no se como contestar. Quieren saber que soy." To my surprise my father, like my mother, answered without hesitation, without inquiring about the circumstances. But unlike her he turned his attention away from what he was doing, his eyes darting in my direction: "Eres India!"

In the kitchen in the English language of my New Mexican mother I was Spanish; in the living room in the Spanish tongue of my Mexican father I was Indian. Clearly something was amiss. I felt as confused as ever, yet I recognized this as one of those taboo subjects that adults appeared to regard as unanswerable and therefore inappropriate. I realized I had asked something whose answer they thought lay beyond my understanding — so I stored it, with other taboo topics, in the hope of enlightenment at a later date. I was Spanish; I was Indian. Mostly I was very confused.

My second story takes place many years later, in the spring of 1986. The University of California at Santa Cruz had awarded me an ethnic studies grant to do preliminary graduate fieldwork in Mexico City. Imagining myself a female Alex Haley, writing my own version of a *Roots* story, I outlined an ethnographic project that aimed at making the personal political and enabled me to trace my late father's footsteps. I would become acquainted with my Mexican kin, tackling what I perceived to be the unsolved mysteries of my father's past and a Mexican tradition that contributed to his unique way of seeing. Because my focus as a graduate student in the History of Consciousness Program had centered primarily on

Anglo-feminist theory, I was convinced that this fieldwork experience would enhance my comprehension of Mexican culture on both sides of the border and my global awareness regarding women's issues.

With a commitment to sharpen my Chicana feminist perceptions and a desire to make this symbolic journey to the "fatherland" memorable, I invited my seventy-eight-year-old mother and my eight-year-old daughter along. I hoped that, unlike the traditional anthropologist, I would be greeted with trust and given an immediate inside view of my Mexican informants' cultural values. My mother and daughter would add their generational perspectives and serve as constant reminders of U.S. attitudes.

During our flight to Mexico City, I noticed subtle changes in my mother's behavior, understandable in light of the fact that we were going to visit my late father's family. The closer we drew to Mexico, the more reserved my mother became. I was well acquainted with the part she was playing and with the subordinate-daughter role required of me. Even so, it was interesting to watch how quickly my mother — a woman who took up swimming at the age of seventy-four; who in her home in California was a spunky, witty, and independent lady, comfortable riding her adult-size tricycle, hanging out with her friends at the senior citizen center, or sitting at home with her favorite new-age health magazine — became a traditional Mexican *viejita*. My daughter, a mestiza of African American, Filipino, and Chicana descent, was unable to categorize her grandmother's behavior. She became so confused and concerned that at one point during the flight she leaned over and whispered, "What's wrong with Grandma?" This simple question unexpectedly revealed the complexity of my ethnographic project; in an instant, I realized that our journey to the "fatherland" would be a transcultural mission that would involve more challenging cultural negotiations than I had anticipated.

The first evening in Mexico City was warmed by our welcome. A number of my cousins — the children and the extended family of our hosts, my *Tio* Lorenzo and *Tia* Esperanza — gathered for dessert and coffee. We visited well into the night, our conversation ranging from current events and updates on family members to memories of my father. My first field notes refer to the number of teenagers actively involved in the discussion, a contrast to my experience in the United States, where adolescents (certainly the ones in my family struggling with the so-called universal issues, where questions of autonomy and generational distinctions sabotage communication) seem to shy away from family gatherings.

This reunion was unlike anything I had envisioned, in that I was quickly positioned as the "native informant" on U.S. values and culture. The high point of the evening came when Tio Lorenzo asked a question that helped crystalize some of the cultural variants beginning to surface between my U.S. and Mexican relatives: "What do you mean by the term *Chicano*?" To my surprise my mother responded (in perfect Spanish) that today Mexicans born in the United States are ashamed of being Mexican and ashamed of being American. In order to move away from a negative self-concept, they use the term *Chicano*. My relatives met these comments with confused expressions and silence, which gave me the opening to say that for me, the term *Chicano* had evolved not so much from shame as from resistance to a belief system in which Americans of Mexican descent are categorized as second-class citizens, as "minorities." This practice, I said, is much like that in Mexico in which U.S.-born Mexicans are labeled *pochos* and viewed in national rather than ethnic/cultural terms. This not fitting in and not being recognized or accepted by the mainstream of either country led them to conclude that the circumstances of their birth carried with them the dubious status of "outsider." To address this problem, the Chicano student movement made a strategic decision to reappropriate the derogatory term *Chicano* and employ it to identify a new political perspective that rejected the second-class status of the hyphenated or so-called Mexican-American. Clearly, it was a matter not of shame but of rejection that led students to resist by fashioning an identity they could call their own.

Tio Lorenzo's face reflected a lack of understanding of U.S. culture, while his reply suggested knowledge of immigration policy and a foreigner's comprehension of the term *American*. "Alvina, you are a woman who has married an American man, doesn't that make you an American?" Aroused by the comment, I snapped back that gender and marriage have little to do with one's ethnic or cultural identity. I still remember how my uncle's rejoinder reminded me of my father's response years earlier to identity questions. Tio Lorenzo spoke knowingly, his answer softened by the smile on his face and the laughter that followed: "Eres feminista!"

"You are Spanish"; "Eres India"; "Eres feminista" — definitive statements that illustrate both my family's assessment of me as a social subject and a Chicana cultural predicament whose very nature inspires creative resistance. That one of these declarations can represent one individual suggests that each option was fashioned for a specific purpose to address a particular challenge. Whenever I (or other Chicanas) attempt to refashion an identity, emphasizing alternative purposes or challenges (I am a "mestiza"; I am a "woman of color"; I am a "Chicana"; "I am a Chicana lesbian"), we involve ourselves in a self-fashioning process that engages someone else's political agenda. Renaming oneself, in this situation, represents a symbolic act of resistance that requires imagination, fluidity, and finesse. The question "What are you?" had made me understand that I was marked as Different. Although my father and mother each answered in their own way, undoubtedly each was reacting to the realities of racism, consciously attempting to fashion an appropriate and fortifying response, identity, or both for their daughter. Stephen Greenblatt's work has shown that self-fashioning is almost always accomplished in relation to something viewed as foreign, strange, or unfriendly; consequently, it is nearly always connected with an experience of threatened injury, damage, or weakening of the self.[2] While at home with my family, I had no desire to compare myself to outsiders, no need to define myself in their terms. As one child among nine, I had simple needs and a limited understanding of the outside world. But my parents, as adults and by virtue of their bilingual/bicultural status, were well versed in U.S. cultural politics. The duality revealed by their responses signals that they were reacting less to my question than to its implications, striving to fashion an identity for me that would withstand the strange and volatile nature of racism.

Interestingly their answers recreate the ancient dichotomy between indigenous and European sensibilities. My father, the more militant of the two, sought to politicize me with "Eres India," while my protective mother provided me with the tools for *passing* — "You are Spanish." Motivated by a parent's love, neither spoke the whole truth; neither considered the bicultural alternative. Their answers reflect the material conditions in which each was socialized. My father, a fair-complexioned native of Mexico City, chose to color himself dark; my olive-complexioned mother, a native of New Mexico, sought identity in European terms. Their contradictory responses reflect a dialectical struggle in self-fashioning that is also reminiscent of two popular strategies for ethnic survival: nationalism and assimilation. My father's Mexican birth and socialization contributed greatly to his cultural pride. My mother, a U.S. citizen by birth, was taught to view her Mexican heritage as a liability. Each attempts to grapple with a form of microaggression encapsulated in the question "What are you?" The very question suggests the interrogator's cultural self-assurance and identification with the mainstream; difference is suspect, abnormal, undesirable.

In my second story, my uncle's answer suggests that gender rather than culture predetermines Chicana difference. My fieldwork experience in Mexico enhanced my awareness that I was not only "a Mexican to Americans, an American to Mexicans," but a woman, a feminist, in both constructions. Because both traditions subordinate and oppress women, Mexicans and Americans alike understand the political implications of feminist cultural resistance. Further, my family's internalization of mainstream attitudes about women or ethnicity also reflect generational and geographical distance.

For example, my mother's socialization in New Mexico undoubtedly influenced her definition of *Chicano*; my definition contrasts dramatically with hers and was influenced by my experiences of living in San Francisco during the 1960s. As women who share a common U.S. birth and ethnic status, my mother and I occupy similar subject positions in the United States. Of different generations, we nevertheless remain aware of our position as outsiders within an Anglo American context.

My uncle's comments expose his patriarchal assumptions about women's roles as much as his pragmatic concerns regarding immigration and national status. As a postcolonial male subject, he equates U.S. status with mobility and privilege. Consider, however,

how quickly he makes the transition from "you are American because you married an American man" to his final judgment — "You
are a feminist."

Theoretically one could approach my anecdotes in a number
of ways. Aside from provoking anxiety, my bilingual, bicultural
experience has enabled me to speak in several languages: Spanish
and English as well as the languages of daughter, mother, and
cultural theorist. Additionally, my representation of the past has
made me painfully aware of the tensions between fact, fiction, and
subjective interpretation. Like an anthropologist, who textualizes
culture by deciding what merits cultural interpretation, a biogra-
pher chooses a central focus, decides what are the "important"
events in an individual's life, then packages the events for consumption in a familiar narrative form that includes a beginning,
middle, and an end. Ethnographers and biographers negotiate
spaces between worlds and sensibilities in order to record the "significant." In my stories, the moves between past and present are
apparent, while the narrative form contains my more subtle mediations between the real and the imaged.

The tension between fact and fiction in some ways resonates
with the anxieties generated by a bilingual, bicultural environment, in that they all ultimately revolve around issues of social
construction and self-fashioning. How does one construct an identity in an alien environment? How does one engage in a writing
project that makes a clear distinction between what is real and
what is imaginary? Rather than examine the fictionality of my
narratives and the limitations of symbolic representation, I would
like to engage in a project of "thick description" focusing on the
published narratives of other women, because I believe that, like
my parents, Chicana storytellers are involved in a process of self-

fashioning.[3] Ultimately their narratives suggest an identity politics that mediates between race, class, and gender.

In this study I am primarily concerned with contemporary Chicana literature written in English. My hope is that *Home Girls* will help bring home the point that Chicano/a culture is the embodiment of multiplicity. I have long admired the way Mario Suarez explains Chicano heterogeneity in his short story "El Hoyo," which he concludes with a creative analogy equating Chicanos with the Mexican dish *capirotada*.

> Its origin is uncertain. But it is made of old, new, stale, and hard bread. It is sprinkled with water and then it is cooked with raisins, olives, onions, tomatoes, peanuts, cheese, and general leftovers of that which is good and bad. It is served hot, cold, or just "on the weather" as they say in El Hoyo. The Garcias like it one way, the Quevedos another, the Trilos another, and the Ortegas still another. While in general appearance it does not differ much from one home to another it tastes different everywhere. Nevertheless it is still *capirotada*. And so it is with El Hoyo's *chicanos*. While many seem to the undiscerning eye to be alike it is only because collectively they are referred to as *chicanos*. But like *capirotada,* fixed in a thousand ways and served on a thousand tables, which can only be evaluated by individual taste, the *chicanos* must be so distinguished.[4]

The writers included in this study, representing different geographical regions, provide readers with a *capirotada* of Chicana perspectives that should dismantle some of the common essentialist misconceptions about Chicana subjectivity. As a classification,

Chicana literature crosses disciplinary boundaries because it unifies the cultural, historical, and literary in a way that forces scholars to confront the limitations of artificial barriers, which compart-
mentalize and contain difference in the name of so-called academic
tradition. The word *Chicana,* for example, signifies a specific ethnic or political identity or both. The term also, by virtue of the final
vowel, denotes female subjectivity. *Literature,* on the other hand,
has come to suggest writing of lasting value and excellence, in verse
or prose. In that it commands an awareness of historical, cultural,
and gender issues, the study of Chicana literature requires an approach that escapes the confines of conservative modes of analysis.[5] When we join the term *Chicana* and *literature* we in fact set
the course for an interdisciplinary exploration of some of the relationships that emerge at the linguistic rendezvous between mainstream and marginal perceptions of literature.

This study should be read as an attempt to interpret Chicana
literature by applying such an interdisciplinary mode of analysis,
which is consistent with the competing and overlapping ideologies
used to interpellate Chicanas in the United States. The project
thus draws upon anthropological, feminist, historical, and literary
sources to examine the writings of Chicana writers, including
Gloria Anzaldúa, Ana Castillo, Denise Chavez, Sandra Cisneros,
and Cherríe Moraga. Representative of a larger group of Chicana
cultural critics, these writers involve themselves with intellectual
projects that interrogate and challenge established tradition. As
revisionists they write in order to inspire social change and influence the future.

Because I am interested in the way Chicana writers creatively
engage literary convention to meet their particular needs, the following chapters range across literary genres — poetry, the short

story, the epistolary novel, *teatro,* and autobiography. My first chapter, "The Politics, Representation, and Emergence of Chicana Aesthetics," establishes a context by focusing on the social and political forces that were significant to an evolving Chicana aesthetics. Chapter two, "Classical Rifts: The Fugue and Chicana Poetics," centers primarily on Chicana discourse. It explores the ways Chicana writers have deployed poetics to address the internal and external limitations imposed by both Anglo American feminist rhetoric and Chicano nationalism. Chapter three, *"The House on Mango Street*: An Appropriation of Word, Space, and Sign,"assesses the ways Sandra Cisneros's cultural, poetic, and prosaic influences contribute to her experimentation with conventions of content and form. Chapter four, "Shades of the Indigenous Ethnographer: Ana Castillo's *Mixquiahuala Letters,*" moves the analysis from the short story to the novel as it explores the relationship between imaginary writing and self-reflexive ethnography. Chapter five, "Orality, Tradition, and Culture in Denise Chavez's *"Novena Narrativas"* and *The Last of the Menu Girls,*" emphasizes performance, domesticity, and oral traditions. The final chapter, "New Visions: Culture, Sexuality, and Autobiography," a synthesis of the preceding chapters, blurs a variety of literary genres by featuring the contributions of two of the most celebrated Chicana writers, Cherríe Moraga and Gloria Anzaldúa.

1

Politics, Representation, and Emergence of Chicana Aesthetics

T aking heed of Fredric Jameson's counsel that one must "always historicize," I begin this study with a brief contextual discussion of the relation of contemporary Chicana literary production to the Chicano renaissance and the 1960s Chicano power movement.[1] Every aspect of this culture and tradition, of course, is rooted in Mexican history, indeed, in the historical processes instigated by the European colonization of the Americas.[2] The intrusion of Spanish colonialists contributed immensely to the schism between indigenous and European traditions. Toppling the icons and cultural symbols of a vibrant Meso-America, replacing them with crosses, statues, and biblical allusions, the Spanish reconstructed the beliefs of the indigenous populations of Mexico.[3] Although the conquistadors intended to strip the native peoples of their faith and values in order to transform them into obedient subjects loyal to Spain, their ferocious entry into the "New World" resulted in interracial relationships and a new heterogeneity described by the term *mestizaje*.[4]

Mexican/Chicano consciousness, like that of other colonized peoples, resonates with a legacy of uncertainty and estrangement. Reflecting on the effects of neocolonialism, Rosa Linda Fregoso maintains that a loss of Mexican territory during the Mexican/American war of 1848 contributed to subsequent waves of immigration to the United States during the twentieth century. Chicano/as have inherited a Mexican history of colonialism and imperialism that subjects them to conquest, marginalization, and domination within their *native* (southwestern) territories.[5] In Fregoso's estimation the Chicano/a social position between Mexican and U.S. cultural establishments epitomizes the carrying forward and across the border of the unresolved conflicts resulting from the invasion and colonization of Mexico. On the positive side, this political dilemma has inspired myriad mediations that contribute to a rich assortment of cultural interpretations.

Chicano literature provides writers with the opportunity to appraise cultural hybridity, or, in Gloria Anzaldúa's terms, to explore "the Borderlands."[6] Although many critics regard Chicano literature as an inclusive or, for that matter, homogeneous category of protest and resistance, this study shifts away from the tendency to emphasize a "generic masculine" sensibility to a focus exclusively on Chicana (women's) writing.

Setting the Theoretical Context

Because it responds to ideological and cultural containment, the production of resistance literature is viewed by Barbara Harlow as a politicized activity. Limiting her focus to gender issues, Julia

Kristeva maintains that female discourse breaks with patriarchal tradition and thus functions as a feminist act of dissidence. Although neither critic makes direct reference to a Chicana predicament, together they illustrate the ways in which cultural containment and female subordination influence Chicana feminist resistance. Harlow and Kristeva enable us to more accurately appraise a Chicana positioning that holds the potential for multiple levels of resistance. To put it in different terms, Harlow and Kristeva provide a foundation for introducing outsiders to the complexities of Chicana existence, and to a mode of literary expression that challenges history as well as the politics of domination.[7]

Before we can fully understand the ways in which Chicana literary production constitutes a challenge, we must determine whom or what it is Chicana writers are compelled to resist. In this context social conditions are of paramount concern because they contribute directly to the kind of alienation and estrangement that motivates aesthetic production.[8] The energy of the 1960s established the momentum for the rise of cultural nationalism as well as a variety of other oppositional movements. Ironically, these independent social movements were legitimized as unified, late in the decade, in spite of their many internal disputes. Some scholars have recognized group fragmentation and division as a natural consequence, yet few push their analysis beyond an acknowledgement of the problem.

Concerning the related issues of power, leverage, and control, Sylvia Harvey suggests that mainstream beliefs suppress the oppositional cultural productions of subordinate classes; rather than obliterate them, dominant ideology works to bring them "within the vast arena of consent which enables a ruling class to assert its authority without the show of naked force."[9] Harvey's dialectical approach highlights the means by which one belief system subordinates or manages another, the rule by which every thought or existing position necessarily creates its opposite. Put simply, dominant ideology poses a challenge that elicits contradictions and counterchallenges from the dominated.

Dialectical criticism enables us to chart the shifting nature of U.S. consciousness and to assess the ways in which the cold-war 1950s, characterized by a patriotic belief in the dominant system, represented the suppression of opposing interests. The 1960s, then, marked an attempt by groups outside the mainstream to end their orchestrated silence. Examining the relationship between the civil rights and women's liberation movements, Jane Bayes describes the dialectical process.

> During the early 1960's, the civil-rights movement, the sit-ins, the freedom rides, and the boycotts occupied national attention and the national media. Many young white women active in the Free Speech Movement, the Student Nonviolent Coordinating Committee, the Students for a Democratic Society, and in various antiwar protest organizations found themselves not only embroiled in the politics of protest but also very cognizant of the fact that second-class status in American society defined not only Black and Brown people but women also. By learning to understand the psychic and political problems of Black people, women came to realize their own psychic imprisonment within traditional institutions and ideologies.[10]

Bayes, insinuating that the containment of difference fuels resistance, enables us to appreciate why the 1950s suppression of U.S. cultural differences contributed to the emergence of a counterhegemonic impulse inspiring the African-American, Asian-American, Mexican-American, and Native-American nationalist agendas that kindled the revival of the white women's movement.[11]

Prioritizing self-determination, most 1960s nationalist ideologies in the United States sought to legitimate their immediate oppositional struggles rather than to build a unified movement against oppression. For instance, despite the global visibility of Third World liberation struggles focused on anti-imperialist ideologies (as in Vietnam, Cuba, and Algeria), African-American, Chicano, Native-American, and Asian-American nationalist movements stressed American ethnic/racial autonomy as they competed for institutional recognition and support. Unfortunately, this political tactic restricted any possibility for appraising the public role of women in liberation struggles. Through a short-sighted assignment of women to clerical or culinary service, cultural nationalist operations helped sow the seeds for internal dissatisfaction and factionalism. To Starhawk's mind, factionalism occurs when political movements challenge patriarchal institutions without questioning the consciousness on which they are founded: "Members may give over their sense of value and content to the 'movement' and then 'burn out' during those periods when it doesn't seem to be moving. Groups divide over questions of dogma, discipline or power and dissipate energy fighting among themselves, attacking friends within the movement rather than enemies."[12] The Chicano power movement's failure to critically examine the patriarchal consciousness of the dominant system led to internal power disputes and to the creation of a cultural nationalism that duplicated the very hierarchical structures it opposed. Chicana women were thus quickly transformed into the subordinate class within Chicano nationalistic literature.[13]

Nationalist aesthetic productions replicated the rhetoric that reified the suppression or omission of female experience(s). Picking up on the lessons learned from the "oppressor," African American, Asian American, Native American, and Chicano/Chicana critics legitimized "minority" cultural productions by constructing alternative literary canons that represented predominantly masculine interpretations of history, ideology, culture. The alternative literature of this historical juncture thus reflected only a partial reality in a way that mimicked the dominant system's marginalization of racialized "minorities."

Overall, the social movements of the 1960s instigated a "dialectics of difference" responsible for new fractures among marginalized groups.[14] Like the Chicano movement, the women's liberation movement, however misinformed or insensitive, was also directly responsible for the emergence of feminist thinking among Chicanas. In this context, Jane Bayes's previous comments illuminate how the essentialist use of the term *women* disregards racial, ethnic, and class differences. Like other "women of color," Chicanas were subordinated and contained by the rhetoric of oppositional movements. On one side they were restrained by the traditional masculine interpretation of their respective cultures and on the other by the dreams and aspirations of a feminist utopian vision that allowed no space for cultural, racial, or, for that matter, class differences among women.[15]

The Chicana Cultural Critic's Social Predicament

Chicana marginality pressures writers either to take one side or the other or to adopt a viewpoint influenced by but not limited to either Anglo-feminist or Chicano ideology. This tenuous stance between opposing ideologies offers Chicana writers new aesthetic opportunities to support or refute either or both of these two oppositional sources and thereby join other feminist activists not only in deconstructing oppressive values but in laying out alternative perspective(s) that represent their social quandary. Gender complicates as it informs a Chicana multiple subjectivity that in turn dramatizes and recasts any previous understanding of cultural *mestizaje*.

The Chicana social predicament necessitates a reconsideration of both the "idealized past" and the "future perfect." This past, a nostalgic interpretation of culture that fails to consider female experience(s), is as oppressive and limiting as the feminists' modernized future, whose liberation is equally confining because it relies on the same old Anglo American values and entrenched social system that have largely failed to consider cultural or ethnic diversity in female experience(s). These "traditional" (masculinist) interpretations of the past and the "progressive" (Anglo-feminist) visions of the future have helped motivate Chicanas to assume a more active role, securing a temporal interlude, the present reality.

With piercing descriptions of contemporary situations, Chicana literature challenges the past/future idealized types of interpretation. In their efforts to contest textual omissions, the writers depict the orality and routine qualities of the rituals and experiences of *familia y mujeres*. When an author represents herself in cultural/feminist terms, she consciously mediates between the dialectical tensions created by the traditional past and modern future opposition, an opposition that takes into account time as well as space. This emergent literary discourse, in this regard, is a mediation of the "Mexican past" and the "American future." Speaking of the folkloric chronotope, Mikhail Bakhtin has shown us that, when taken out of its relationship to the past and future, "the present loses its integrity, breaks down into isolated phenomena and objects, making of them a mere abstract conglomeration."[16] Gloria Anzaldúa illuminates Bakhtin's point with her discussion of the tensions that inform her "present" relationship to the past and future:

> The mixture of bloods and affinities, rather than confusing or unbalancing me, has forced me to achieve a kind of equilibrium. Both cultures deny me a place in their universe . . . I walk the tightrope with ease and grace. I span abysses. Blindfolded in the blue air. The sword between my thighs, the blade warm with my flesh. I walk the rope — an acrobat in equipoise, expert at the Balancing Act.[17]

Anzaldúa's poetic depiction of her mediation process, the "balancing act" between ideological systems, epitomizes the Chicana writer's dilemma. Because Mexican and American cultures eclipse Chicana subjectivity, both contribute to a loss of self that fuels the Chicana writer's urgency to reject "old" contradictions in order to create "new," relevant identity affiliations. This tenuous stance between opposing ideologies unleashes the writer's need to understand the relationship between different histories — to take into account the totality.

Chicana Literary Criticism

Aside from a variety of anthologized essays, only three book-length studies critically analyze literary works by or about Chicanas: Cordelia Candelaria's *Chicano Poetry: A Critical Introduction,* Ramón Saldívar's *Chicano Narrative: Dialectics of Difference,* and Marta Sánchez's *Contemporary Chicana Poetry: A Critical Approach to an Emerging Literature.* The studies by Sánchez and Candelaria serve as solid introductions that can be characterized by their descriptive/structural concerns on the one hand, and on the other by their allegiance to either Anglo American feminist or Chicano nationalist ideologies. Consequently they reproduce many of the problems associated with exclusivity.

Marta Sánchez thinks of her work, *Contemporary Chicana Poetry: A Critical Approach to an Emerging Literature,* the first book-length study of Chicana poetry, "not as a full-fledged theory" but as an attempt to lay the foundation necessary for reading and interpreting Chicana poetry. Focusing on four contemporary Chicana poets — Alma Villanueva, Lorna Dee Cervantes, Lucha Corpi, and Bernice Zamora — Sánchez has helped fill the void created by a U.S. literary tradition that had either disregarded or suppressed an emerging body of literature representative of the fastest growing ethnic group in the nation.

Sánchez places Chicana poetry in the historical context of the 1970s, outlining the factors that influence a culture and, by the same token, a literature that draws from both Anglo American and Mexican traditions. In the introductory chapter Sánchez also outlines the external forces that sustain the demarcation of social formations and cultural difference(s) in the United States. Within a framework that exposes a Chicana social predicament marked by a double set of tensions between values and culture, ethnicity and gender, Sánchez argues convincingly that Chicana poetics is inspired by conflict and struggle. She dramatizes these tensions with a theoretical paradigm of the affiliations — Woman, Chicana, and Poet—available to Chicana poets. "The tensions among the three identities," Sánchez explains, "are localized between different points of the triad: between 'woman' and 'Chicana;' between 'woman' and 'male;' between 'Chicana' and 'Chicano;' between 'Chicana poet' and 'English-American poet;' between 'woman poet' and 'Mexican poet' between 'Chicana poet' and 'Chicano poet.'"[18] From this paradigm, Sánchez defines the social predicament in which Chicanas find themselves as citizens of the United States.

Although Sánchez's structuralist approach illustrates the oppositional tensions that confront Chicana poets, it subverts any discussion of multiple subjectivity or its political implications. Sánchez is thus free to conclude, for example, that Alma Villanueva responds primarily as a woman struggling in the patriarchal U.S. setting; that Lorna Dee Cervantes reacts as a Chicana grappling with her role as poet; that Lucha Corpi, categorized as a sexually repressed and confused woman, defines herself in relation to traditional Mexican society; and that Bernice Zamora responds either as a Chicana woman or as a poet, "but seldom as both." Sánchez's literary paradigm thereby aligns with an essentialist, early women's-studies agenda and ultimately reveals more about her own preferences and influences than those of the poets in question. Her emphasis on the themes that gender oppression motivates limits her analysis of the political concerns and aesthetics of Chicano cultural nationalism.

Cordelia Candelaria's *Chicano Poetry: A Critical Introduction* begins with an even more detailed historical overview of Chicano culture and literature. In this ambitious study, Candelaria attempts a comprehensive survey of the poetry by paying homage to the prominent writers who helped establish the foundation for Chicano poetic expression. Her text provides a teleological model of the evolution of Chicano poetics based on a conservative, canonical interpretation of form and style. Because this too is an introductory text intended to outline Chicano poetry in a systematic fashion, Candelaria employs a structuralist approach that rings of formalist and descriptive analysis. The limitations of this approach rather than Candelaria's skill as a literary critic account for a tendency to mystify Chicano/a creative expression. Here, as in the case of Sánchez, the structuralist/formalist method functions to contain the political, as it suppresses any discussion of ideological tensions.

Candelaria emphasizes form and theme and what she identifies as the natural logic of a poetic formation to divide Chicano poetry into three evolutionary phases. Phase one, characterized by the rhetoric of opposition and labeled a basic or crude poetics, has two major themes. The first foregrounds binary oppositions, functions of the us/them polarity as represented by the concept of internal colonialism. "The other central phase one theme concerns raza [race] identity — its nature, its recovery from under layers of colonialist wrappings, its definition and its redefinition."[19] In phase two, the basic elements of Chicano poetics are established — language, symbolism, and ritual. Candelaria suggests that the poetics of this stage, more complex on a thematic and stylistic level, transcends the movement or protest poetry of phase one; "It is the work of these Phase two poets which led directly and forcefully to a *genuine* Chicano poetics" (130, emphasis mine). Phase three, the most advanced, Candelaria describes as an elegant and genteel period of Chicano poetics. Its poetry reveals "sophistication of style & technique," an individuality in treatment of subject and theme, and the kind of skill and control that "signal an inevitably developed form — much as the vivid blossoms of a cactus inevitably flower out of the spiny base" (137). Here Candelaria identifies a "genuine" Chicano canon based on subjectivity and an inward turning in search of the lyrical poetic self.

Although Candelaria concentrates more intensely on women writers in her discussion of phase three, by comparing Walt Whitman to Chicana poets Bernice Zamora, Lorna Dee Cervantes, and Inés Tovar she subordinates Chicana poetry as she legitimates it by tying it to the predominantly masculine Anglo American canonical tradition.[20] With this linkage she inadvertently invites an ironic reading of Chicano/a poetics, since her summary of Chicano history had credited the Chicano renaissance with developing a literary expression that contradicted dominant Western modes of perception. Candelaria's analysis sends a powerful ideological message of containment; she uses the dominant canonical system to evaluate and legitimize an oppositional mode of creative expression.

While Marta Sánchez devotes an entire text to understanding the tensions created for Chicana poets among the roles in the Woman/Chicana/Poet triad she perceives, Candelaria suppresses feminist difference(s) and thus denies any perception of Chicana alienation and estrangement from Chicano and Anglo American oppositional ideologies. In their alternative approaches to Chicana poetry, Sánchez and Candelaria consequently underscore important rhetorical differences that distinguish female and feminist ideological perspectives.

Historian Linda Gordon makes a clear distinction between the female and the feminist that helps us understand the difficulties confronting Sánchez and Candelaria as they surveyed Chicana poets and tried to develop universal interpretive tools for appreciating Chicana poetic expression. Gordon explores the "inescapable tension" between the natural and the political experience of women:

> Throughout various parts of feminist scholarship today there is an attempt to reach a false resolution of [that] tension . . . a resolution that would obliterate the distinction between the female and the feminist. It seems to me important to claim both. The female is ourselves, our bodies and our socially constructed experience. It is not the same as feminism, which is not a "natural" exertion of that experience but a controversial political interpretation and struggle, by no means universal to women.[21]

Given this formulation, Candelaria emphasizes female qualities whereas Sánchez builds a literary paradigm firmly grounded on feminist principles. These two critics, like the Chicana writers they address, are grappling with the recurrent female/feminist dilemma, developing theoretical texts that underscore the importance of launching an analysis that articulates both perspectives, a synthesis that obliterates the distinction.

By bringing forth readings that foreground female/feminist perspectives in Chicano/a cultural production, Sánchez and Candelaria provide a challenging context for other critics to conduct an ideological analysis of the literature. In Raymond Williams's terms, this analytic project needs to demonstrate how "the facts of alternative and oppositional forms of social life and culture, in relation to the effective and dominant culture," are subject to historical variation and are significant sources of information about the dominant culture itself.[22]

The third study, Ramón Saldívar's *Chicano Narrative: The Di-*

alectics of Difference, insinuates that before we attempt to theorize about Chicana literature we should make ourselves aware of the ideological tensions that have inspired it. "If Chicano narrative is, as we have claimed throughout this study, a perfect case study of the work of ideologies that are not simply counter hegemonic but truly oppositional and revolutionary, then the literature produced by Chicana authors is counterhegemonic to the second power, serving as a critique of critiques of oppression that fail to take into account the full range of domination."[23] Saldívar thus cautions us to take into account the concrete reality that gave rise to Chicana aesthetics, just as Sylvia Harvey warns that a theory of cultural production is incomplete without an awareness of the "specific aesthetic and institutional forms which it seeks to analyze and then to reconstruct."[24] Because "minority" women are interpellated by a series of competing and overlapping ideologies, we should view their artistic endeavors as emerging from a complex material reality influenced by race, class, ethnicity, gender, national origin, and education. Speaking of the writing of the powerless, bell hooks maintains that writing produced by any exploited or colonized group should be recognized for its creative resistance as well as its creative expression.[25] An analysis that confines its focus to artistic/creative expression can at best establish alternative canonical systems based on dominant aesthetic forms and institutions. In recognizing these complexities, we begin to see how employing an ideological approach that examines both the historical and the aesthetic might minimize the risk of reducing our analysis to celebratory and descriptive readings of art.

With an ideological analysis of Chicana creative expression as foreground, this study aspires to contribute to the discussion initiated by Marta Sánchez and Cordelia Candelaria. In addition, in it I accept Ramón Saldívar's invitation to consider "the most vibrant new development in Chicano literature, the emergence of a significant body of works by women authors in the 1970s and 1980s."[26] A sustained analysis of the literary production of Chicanas then provides a basis for reflecting on form and genre as historical by-products of a perspective formed in relationship to both Mexican and American culture. In the following pages I survey both poetic and narrative voices of an emergent Chicana literary enterprise to develop an analysis that will enable us to move beyond a celebratory interpretation that merely identifies the presence of women's voices.

2

Classical Rifts:
The Fugue and Chicana Poetics

Many feminist critics now recognize the weakness of a theoretical perspective that focuses on the contrasts between men and women rather than on the differences among women. Male/female binary oppositions do little more than aggravate the discord that leads women of color to challenge feminist discourse for making "universal" claims that are based on an assumption of white, Eurocentric privilege.[1] Marilyn Strathern's estimation of the importance of feminist debate is useful in this context. For her, feminist debate serves to maintain a solid feminist connection; consequently what appears to be an impossible array of conflicting theoretical perspectives should more appropriately be viewed as a multiplicity of voices and positions that are set explicitly in relation to one another.[2] In light of the differences that sustain feminist theorists writing today, Strathern's point is well taken, but how does it apply to women of color, who tend to avoid abstract theorizing or claims that their own theoretical insights are universal?

Dominated by patriarchal notions, mainstream ideology shores up the authority that men have over the roles and status of women in society. In an effort to remedy masculinist domination, feminist theorists have appropriately begun to develop discourse(s) that address issues related to the subordination and control of women. Since, in many instances, the voices of women of color remain unrepresented in this "array of theoretical positions," they have become a suppressed text relegated to the margins of feminist rhetoric.[3]

The sociological category "marginal person" describes a social reality characterized by constant negotiation between two or more cultural systems.[4] Although Chicanas are familiar with the marginal position allocated to racialized ethnic minorities in the United States, the gender constraints that complicate their marginal subjectivity often remain suppressed, denied, or overlooked by the dominant cultural systems on both sides of the U.S.-Mexican border. Aside from compounding marginality, the so-called universal attitude concerning the unimportance of gender contributes to new sites of Chicana social conflict and cultural ambiguity. Ironically, patriarchal attitudes often create new tensions between culture and gender that reinforce Chicana indifference toward the women's movement and feminist theory. In this chapter I seek to expand upon Strathern's discussion of the gender limitations perpetuated by traditional academic disciplines by considering the tensions between Anglo and Chicana feminist perspectives rather than the problems that arise as a result of conservative academic practices. Because Chicana writers take a variety of narrative approaches to articulate their subjective reflections, we need to examine different forms of writing as alternatives to abstract theorization.[5] Rather than simply dismissing Chicana creative writers by labeling them as "passive," "descriptive," or "non-theoretical" (judgments that privilege a particular type of writing), I would like to spend some time considering literary production. If Chicana writers are drawn to poetic forms, it seems obvious that we should turn our attention to poetry. We must bear in mind what is available and interpret the abundant poetic forms rather than simply preoccupy ourselves with what some perceive as theoretical scarcity. We must, in short, acknowledge the relevance and importance of other forms of cultural articulations.

Poetry provides Chicanas with the vehicle to voice female concerns much in the way the dominant ideology of the United States provides the medium for male discourse.[6] As Adrienne Rich points out: "A radical critique of literature, feminist in its impulse, would take the work first of all as a clue to how we live, how we have been living, how we have been led to imagine ourselves, how our language has trapped as well as liberated us; and how we can begin to see — and therefore live — afresh." [7]

Poetics as Theory

By relying strictly on the parameters set by conventional academic discourse, some feminist theorists have fallen prey to the notion that science or theory must remain separate from art. Alison Jaggar, for example, dismisses the contributions of women of color:

A relatively small body of written work is available by feminists of color other than black feminists, and what is available is mainly at the level of *description*. Of course, a fully adequate theory of women's liberation cannot ignore the experience of any group of women and, to the extent that socialist feminism fails to theorize the experience of women of color, it cannot be accepted as complete. So far, however, relatively few attempts exist by non-black feminists of color to develop a *distinctive and comprehensive theory* of women's liberation.[8] (emphasis mine)

When feminist theorists move away from binary conceptualizations like Jaggar's that equate literary production with fiction or description and abstract theoretical writing with truth, when they examine more closely the relationship between description and theory, they will open the doors to more comprehensive theorizing about cultures and individuals.

Regarding the social scientific method, Susan Krieger observes:

Our models are not only abstract, but also out of touch. I think that descriptive explanations, with their primary faithfulness to data and detail, are one way to break out of this pattern, to show more of what is "really" going on. They require a combination of the novelist's and the social scientist's mind: a willingness to construct a representation as a novelist might, yet at the same time a desire to think like a social scientist.[9]

As one of the early voices for interdisciplinary studies, Krieger describes a methodology that has only recently come to fruition within the academy in the form of cultural studies. If we wish to move feminist theorizing beyond intellectual calisthenics, knowledge should be applied across the disciplines, intertwined, woven into life experiences, so that it will amount to more than compartmentalized, bite-sized bits of information for the exclusive consumption of a particular academic audience.

The problems that arise from traditional approaches to theory represent yet another aspect of the ongoing debate over the relative merits of scientific observation and descriptive interpretation. Although Clifford Geertz's comments on the interpretation of cultures avoid any consideration of women, Geertz does provide a convincing and eloquent argument for "thick description" as a means of moving anthropology beyond subjective abstract data and analysis to the semiotic interpretation generally employed by literary critics. Thus, Geertz's position is not far from Krieger's. Speaking as a literary theorist, Terry Eagleton contributes to this discussion by suggesting that "science gives us conceptual knowledge of a situation, [and] art gives us the experience of that situation, which is equivalent to ideology. But by doing this, it allows us to 'see' the nature of that ideology, and thus begins to move us towards that full understanding of ideology which is scientific knowledge."[10] Acknowledging the interconnection between actual human behavior and its symbolic representation sets the stage for a more inclusive type of theorizing that will eventually eliminate the ineffective, outdated, and above all inaccurate kind of analysis that limits many feminist scholars today.

A form of ethnography, women's literature provides the method, voices, experiences, and rituals of growing up female. Like ethnographers, Chicana writers focus on microcosms within a culture, unpacking rituals in the context of inherited symbolic and social structures of subjugation. They use their own writing for self-analysis; their cultural self-ethnographies or self-representations provide an indispensable means for deconstructing Chicana cultural experience(s), because they eliminate the possibility of outside misinterpretation of cultural symbolic systems and allow the writer to record an intimate social discourse regarding her ambivalence around ethnicity and gender. This process permits marginal individuals to become the subjects of their own discourse.

When a female child is born to Mexican parents living in the United States, she becomes more than *daughter* in the abstract sense of the term; rather she, like other female babies, is viewed as her mother's daughter, a chip off the old female block so to speak. Because gender determines the way descendants are socialized, we understand how females born into this world are also more than their mothers' daughters; they are the daughters of the ideology of their time.[11] Women first, Mexicans second—they are female manchildren of the world in which they live, destined to search for cultural identification and meaning based on their gender.

Freud asked, "What do women want?" Women continue to ask in various ways, "Who are we?" Forced to exist in a vacuum within a male-defined world, women challenge tradition in order to survive. And every time the familiar question of identity resurfaces, new questions arise, new developments occur. In universities, through feminist and other scholarly theories, women begin to understand that they are historical creatures.[12] This realization should not be dismissed as insignificant or obvious, for once women examine their historicity in terms of fashioning a specific identity, they are well on the way to confronting the kinds of limitations that have maintained their subordinate status.

As an ideological production that mirrors Chicana multiple subjectivity, Chicana literature similarly challenges many of the cultural limitations placed on women and furnishes a key to unlocking the mysteries surrounding Chicana experience(s). It thus functions as an allegory of the Chicana social dilemma. Chicana poetics resembles the feminist voices of Anglo American women in that Chicanas' political perspectives often appear to be, in Marilyn Strathern's words, "in constant debate." Considering Chicana poetic production as a totality, a cultural apparatus in itself, should place us in a better position to understand the intricacies of the debate.

In my eyes the entire Chicana literary text is analogous to a musical fugue; both employ polyphony, with separate voices maintaining comparative integrity throughout a composition.

A fugue begins with a theme, or "subject," on which each voice enters in turn, as if "imitating" the preceding one. Each voice follows the subject with a "countersubject." The opening, called the "exposition," introduces the main material and all the voices. Then comes a "development," in which there are many "episodes," introducing new material, playing the voices against each other in various combinations, transforming the themes rhythmically and harmonically, taking the music far from the opening key or tonality.[13]

Opening on an apologetic note, Chicana poetics rely heavily on the pitch set by cultural or religious ideologies. Once this tonality has set the mood, establishing how Chicanas position and identify themselves in cultural terms, it is followed by the counterpoint voices of rage and opposition. The development caused by the interchange of these two modes introduces new material as it transforms the original theme; Chicana poetic discourse moves further in search of a knowledge of "self" in oppositional terms. Out of this opposition new themes of struggle and identification emerge; the overall tone shifts from disempowered marginal subjects to self-sufficient women at the center. In rhythm and counterrhythm, the voices continue to thrive, propelled into the self-reflexive terrain of the literature of new vision.[14]

This new-vision modality, which focuses on broader issues dealing with survival of the species and culture as well as issues related to a concept I call the "universal woman," is not final but marks only another layer in the quest for self-fashioning and analytical comprehension. The literature at this stage, self-conscious and self-critical, often offers more questions than answers, interpreting, drawing from, and resonating with the earlier modes in the literary discourse. In this sense the stage of new vision functions as the springboard to a more global discussion of the gender/culture dichotomy, as it attempts to crystallize the Chicana necessity for cultural and feminist identification.

Literature of the new-vision interval generally involves moving beyond culturally bound analysis to more transformative, universal issues concerning the subordination of women in general.

Helene Cixous's "The Laugh of the Medusa" yields a notion of the universal woman that alludes to the fervor augmenting women's creativity and the literature of new vision. This concept speaks to the need for women to develop a discourse: "Woman must put herself into the text—as into the world and into history—by her own movement," says Cixous.

> I've seen them, those who will be neither dupe nor domestic, those who will not fear the risk of being a woman; will not fear any risk, any desire, any space still unexplored in themselves, among themselves and others or anywhere else. They do not fetishize, they do not deny, they do not hate. They observe, they approach, they try to see the other woman, the child, the lover—not to strengthen their own narcissism or verify the solidity or weakness of the master, but to make love better, to invent.[15]

On an existential level, this passage echoes the concerns of many women of color. Chicanas for the most part have supported any movement that criticizes the need to improve oneself by denigrating others. Cixous outlines an all-encompassing utopian method for mobilizing all women toward a universal concept of womanhood under the unifying issues that revolve around sexism. Her rhetoric exemplifies a consciousness to which many women aspire yet at the same time excludes a significant number of women, for it fails to acknowledge race, ethnicity, and class as overdetermining factors. Nevertheless, simply by illuminating the paradox, Cixous takes a step toward a final resolution of the conflict between white women and women of color, since the evolved consciousness she proposes can only be achieved after women begin to critically address the implicit contradictions in her argument.

Marilyn Strathern's discussion concerning the relationship between feminist perspectives becomes all the more meaningful when we interrogate the problems Cixous's contention raises for women of color and explore the discursive connection between these opposing perspectives. Seen in this way, we understand how the limitations of Cixous's theoretical construct provoke debate and new awareness that contribute to the development of a more global feminist discourse; we understand that in the final analysis, we cannot speak about universal notions without first acknowledging our differences. Like Cixous, Chicana poetry generates discussion.

In this light, my questions of Chicana literature attend to how it produces meaning. How do the stories and poetry of Chicana writers develop a new framework from which to view women? Does Chicana literature present an alternative perspective or the kind of cultural intervention Annette Kuhn describes as a subversion of and challenge to "mainstream texts"?[16]

Chicana Poetics:
From Apology to New Vision

I have delineated four modes of Chicana literature: apology, rage and opposition, struggle and identification, and new vision. (In contrast, Thomas Ybarra, in a linear/historical reading of the literary text, has divided the Chicano literary process into three stages: genesis, subversion, and regeneration. His final stage does, however, include what he calls the evolution of Chicana feminist thought based on the politics of language and colonization.) The provocative question to ask regarding the new-vision mode or stage, which includes this historical moment, concerns the relationship of literary form to modes of production, for in Fredric Jameson's view of dialectical thinking, "aesthetic objects can only come into existence through a process of alienation and estrangement within human society." Not until the late 1970s and early 1980s (a period that coincided with the solidification of the second wave of the women's movement in the United States) did women's views begin appearing "en masse" in the literature regarding the politics of language and colonization.[17]

The first mode I have identified, the literature of apology, is liberal in the sense that it develops the argument that traditions and cultural values kept women from developing to their full potential. Although Ybarra has included the literature of this interval in his final stage-regeneration, the term *reappropriation* more accurately describes this movement, which is a reclamation of history as opposed to the rebirthing of a literature that until this historical moment, was virtually nonexistent. The works of this period mark a significant feminist reappropriation of history as they subvert the Chicano historical text through justifications or radical explanations. Such literature underscores the power of language to subordinate, for it emphasizes the struggle for assimilation, which is primarily accomplished by acquiesing to a language and discourse outside of the Chicano/a culture. This attitude is expressed in Lorna Dee Cervantes' poem "Refugee Ship":

> Like wet cornstarch, I slide
> past my grandmother's eyes. Bible
> at her side, she removes her glasses.
> The pudding thickens.
> Mama raised me without language.
> I'm orphaned from my Spanish name.
> The words are foreign, stumbling
> on my tongue. I see in the mirror
> my reflection: bronzed skin, black hair.
> I feel I am a captive
> aboard the refugee ship.
> The ship that will never dock.
> *El barco que nunca atraca.*[18]

Cervantes describes the alienation process, which begins with feelings of isolation or orphanhood from a name, creeps in through the cracks of the bicultural experience, and ultimately robs many Chicanas of a crucial part of their identity, reducing their language to foreign words that stumble on the tongue.[19]

The literature of apology attempts to deconstruct myth and dominant codes in order to liberate women. Once the mood or theme has been set, as in a musical fugue, new voices join in, repeating the initial theme and introducing different, sharper intervals or counterrhythms, new definitions of woman, reinterpreting the history and myth that have held women captive. These new Chicana voices begin to reappropriate historical figures predominantly represented by masculine discourse, to politely challenge, for example, the use of the virgin/whore dichotomy brought about largely by male domination and interpretation of ideology, history, and language. Here is Lucha Corpi's "Marina Virgin" . . .

> Of her own accord, before the altar
> of the crucified god she knelt.
> Because she loved you, she only saw
> the bleeding man, and loved in him
> her secret and mourning memory of you.[20]

Corpi's poem refers to the indigenous woman Malintzin Tenepal, whom the conquistadors called Doña Marina and Mexican historians have labeled La Malinche (the Evil One) because of her role in the Conquest as Hernán Cortés's translator, thus as the "whore" responsible for the Spaniards' victory. By questioning the label, Lucha Corpi attempts to undermine the negative position Marina has been given in historical accounts. The poem's title, "Marina Virgin," is the first indication of her oppositional stance. In subtle language packed with religious allusions that reflect her own acceptance of Catholic ideology, Corpi offers a logical rationale for Marina's role, reinscribing her, in an apologetic tone, as the innocent, faithful, loving disciple.

The second mode I have defined, the literature of rage and opposition, is characterized by a feminism confident and bold in tone, no longer apologizing or rationalizing away women's inequality but rather challenging and demanding equal rights for women. The ideals of this radical feminism correspond to those emphasized by the "New Left" Alison Jaggar describes in *Feminist Politics And Human Nature*.[21] Numerous Chicanas write in this mode, passionately denouncing the Chicano's use of *la mujer* and even the *movimiento* for his own ends. In "You Cramp My Style, Baby," typical of the poetry of this period, Lorna Dee Cervantes denounces the sexual exploitation of woman glorified in the name of tradition and glossed over by the *raza* rhetoric:

> You cramp my style, baby
> when you roll on top of me
> shouting, "Viva La Raza"
> at the top of your prick.
> You want me como un taco,
> dripping grease,
> or squeezing maza through my legs,
> making tamales for you out of my daughters.
> You "mija"
> "mija" "mija" me
> until I can scream
> and then you tell me,
> "Esa, I LOVE
> this revolution!
> Come on Malinche,
> gimme some more!"[22]

The literature of rage and opposition is grounded in revolutionary rhetoric, its stinging expression directly confronting rather than circling the issues of female exploitation. Its purpose is to renounce and overthrow masculine domination, to move the Chicana from sexual subjugation to liberation. This mode virtually ignores economic, social, and racial exploitation, concerning itself almost exclusively with the sexual.

Writer and social activist Cherríe Moraga works within the mode of rage and opposition; her sharp-edged writing (essays, plays, poetry, and short stories) openly questions the role of men in Chicano culture. In "Lo Que Nunca Paso Por Sus Labios," Moraga writes of the institution of heterosexuality and its side effect, heterosexism. Primarily concerned with sexuality, her work departs from traditional radical feminist form in its emphasis on ethnicity and culture:

> Chicanas' negative perceptions of ourselves as sexual persons and our consequential betrayal of each other finds its roots in a four-hundred year long Mexican history and mythology. It is further entrenched by a system of anglo imperialism which long ago put Mexicanos and Chicanos in a defensive posture against the dominant culture. The sexual legacy passed down to the Mexicana/ Chicana is the legacy of betrayal, pivoting around the historical/mythical female figure of Malintzin Tenepal. As translator and strategic advisor and mistress to the Spanish conqueror of Mexico, Hernán Cortéz, Malintzin is considered the mother of the mestizo people. But unlike La Virgen de Guadalupe, she is not revered as the Virgin Mother, but rather slandered as La Chingada, meaning the "fucked one," or La Vendida, sell-out to the white race.[23]

As Terry Eagleton reminds us, "Literary works are not mysteriously inspired, or explicable simply in terms of their author's psychology. They are forms of perception, particular ways of seeing the world; and as such they have a relation to that dominant way of seeing the world which is the social mentality or ideology of an age."[24] Moraga's provocative contribution to feminist literature attempts to free Chicanas from the phallocentric literature of the 1960s. Her work ruptures some of the myths and taboos that until recently have gone unchallenged, tucked away under a very intricately sewn cultural cloak. Joining the ranks of other radical writers of protest and liberation, she uses her literary skills to help bridge the gap between the literature of apology and the literature of struggle and identification.

In the literature of struggle and identification writers are not preoccupied with the definition by negation of the literature of apology or the definition by reversal of the literature of opposition. Taking to heart the implications of Marxist theory, this mode of the literature brings women to the forefront as productive, self-sufficient, and complex human beings in their own right.

Gina Valdes's *There Are No Madmen Here,* a wonderful example, recounts the life of Maria Portillo, a stereotypical Mexican woman exploited by her husband, lonely, insecure, and frustrated in her traditional role of wife and mother. Maria's feelings and emotions often leave her questioning:

> She had not done what she wanted for so long that she was not sure of what she really wanted, but she knew that it was something other, better than what she had. She felt tired of thinking, of looking for work, of not finding it, of trying to figure out her husband's moods and whereabouts, of waiting for him. At night, lying on the edge of the double bed, she often felt alone, more so than when she had been a single woman.

She finds herself caught between staying in her traditional role, lonely and unfulfilled, or pulling out and taking control of her life. Valdes's protagonist decides to take her life into her own hands by moving to the United States with her three daughters. The novelette makes a strong statement about the will and determination of this mother confronted with the frustration of dealing with a foreign country and language. On one level, the story is about oppression and Maria's struggle for survival, but in a larger perspective it is about the marginalization of a people. Valdes also develops a subversive subtext to emphasize the tension between tradition and modernity that many postcolonial novelists have grappled with. As Maria watches her family begin to vacillate between cultures, Valdes poses a riddle that focuses the issue:

> "Did you hear what she said? She's ten years old and she can't speak English." "Why should I speak English? I'm Mexican." "You live in the United States, you should speak English." "I don't live here, I'm visiting." "Visiting? You've been visiting for three years." "At least I speak English better than you speak Spanish. What kind of Mexican are you?" "I'm not Mexican, I'm American, and so are you, we were born here." Maria saw her young niece running to her mother. "Mama! Louie says that I'm American because I was born here. Is that true?" "Tell me, mijita, if the kittens are born in the oven, are they kittens? Or are they biscuits?"[25]

Madmen focuses on Maria as head of household, managing her life, working so that her daughters will have a better time of it. In a sense, this is a success story: Maria abandons her husband and her role of subordinate wife. But Maria's liberation leaves a lot to be desired because, as she soon discovers, in the United States her ethnicity, class, and gender are liabilities. Maria's job in a sewing factory pays badly, and she supplements her income by working in the family's tequila-smuggling business. And although she has escaped one man, she hangs on tightly to Saint Anthony, Saint Jude, the Pope, and of course the Almighty Father. She remains powerless not because of her macho husband but because of the capitalistic system of production and corruption, which is directly related to the religious system that subordinates her. The two institutions form an iron-clad social order that traps Maria in a life of inequality.

Gina Valdes's work often invites women to take a look at the broader picture, to assess levels of exploitation and discrimination by asking what is at stake. Valdes's poem "Working Women" addresses some of the same issues that appear in *Madmen*.

> Mi amigo, un cholo transplantado,
> anda todo alocado con su Monte Carlo
> amarillo con swivel bucket seats,
> sun roof y quadraphonic sounds.
> Me lleva low riding por El Cajon
> a mirujear a las rucas on display
> this working night, una con sus
> tight red pants boogying on the curb,
> fast gone, una gordita con su little
> skirt hasta el ombligo y su fake fur,
> otras dos waiting sentadas for a trick,
> y el chota con sus two fast guns
> acercándoseles a otras dos, y ahí into
> Winchell's Donuts entra el pimp con

sus red pants, white shirt y su
cocked felt hat, y yo no se que ando
aquí cruising so low, mirujeando
this working women's scene, thinking
of what rucas and rucos do to pay
their rent and eat, I, a poet hustling
hot verbs, a teacher selling brainwaves
in the S.D. red light school district,
feeling only un poco mejor than these
rucas of the night, a little luckier,
just as worn, my ass grinded daily
in this big cathouse U S A, que a
todos nos USA, una puta más in this
prostitution ring led by a heartless
cowboy pimp.[26]

The poem characterizes the untenable position Chicanas find themselves in as they maneuver between Mexican and Anglo-American cultures. Although the negative side of this experience sometimes leads (as Lorna Dee Cervantes's poem "Refugee Ship" suggests) to feelings of isolation and alienation from the Spanish language, on the other, more positive side of the bicultural experience lies the opportunity to experiment with two languages. The Chicana's marginal positioning between cultures requires working within two code systems. Valdes' poem beautifully illustrates how code switching is a type of verbal interaction characteristic of bilingual populations in the midst of social change. But her poem moves far beyond code switching as it demonstrates the irony and limitations of a system that either subordinates or reifies its subject population.

The final category in my scheme, the literature of new vision, welcomes multiple voices and viewpoints as it extracts elements of all of the former intervals. I chose the term *new vision* because of the broader transformative view of this body of work. Rather than limiting themselves to single forms of oppression, these works speak to a number of social problems, without taking an authoritarian tone or dictating a particular perspective. The varied Chicana voices in this mode speak, as Strathern states, "in relation to one another," pointing to an "array of theoretical positions." Together they hold the possibility for real social change and transformation.

Here Chicana and Chicano writing part ways. The three categories into which Tomás Rivera divided Chicano literature (conversation that records and preserves deeds and people; rebellion and conflict; and invention and creation) apply only to Chicano writing. Juan Felipe Herrera clarifies the difference when he recognizes Chicana feminist literature as "the most visible and vital branch in contemporary Raza writing" and contrasts it to the conservative tendencies of Chicano writers who have been recognized and subsequently included in college curriculums. They have as a result become comfortable and "opted for the cool intellectualism typical of the North American literary voice, with hopes of accommodation by East coast publishing centers."[27] Because this recognition has come at the expense of the feminine interpretation of history, the acceptance or legitimation of Chicano writers by academia works to contain Chicana writers. And because Chicana writers continue to run up against the limits imposed on them by this Chicano interpretation of history, they are still writing with desire, still struggling against oppression. Theirs thus remains a literature of passion and rebellion.

For Chicanas, writing brings power as it signals change. Cherríe Moraga speaks of the power of language in "It's the Poverty" . . .

> I lack imagination you say.
> No. I lack language.
> The language to clarify
> my resistance to the literate.
> Words are a war to me.
> They threaten my family.
> To gain the word
> to describe the loss
> I risk losing everything.
> I may create a monster
> the word's length and body
> swelling up colorful and thrilling
> looming over my mother, characterized.
> Her voice in the distance
> unintelligible illiterate.
> These are the monster's words.[28]

Moraga illustrates what is at stake when Chicanas speak out, unmasking the rewards as well as the penalties that come with the articulation of ideas.

In its underscoring of the burden of the oppressed, Moraga's poetic discourse brings to mind Paulo Freire's contention in *Pedagogy of the Oppressed* that the central conflict for the oppressed lies in:

the choice between being wholly themselves or being divided; between ejecting the oppressor within or not ejecting him; between human solidarity or alienation; between following prescriptions or having choices; between being spectators or actors; between acting or having the illusion of acting through the action of the oppressors; between speaking out or being silent, castrated in their power to create and re-create, in their power to transform the world.[29]

Like Freire, Cherríe Moraga raises questions regarding the oppressed; more important, her interrogations pierce the limitations of the masculinist ideology Freire aligns himself with that equates testicles with power.

Considering power in a different way, Sandra Cisneros writes about its relationship to writing and liberation in *The House on Mango Street*:

She listened to every book, every poem I read her. One day I read her one of my own. I came very close. I whispered it into the pillow:

> I want to be
> like the waves on the sea,
> like the clouds in the wind,
> but I'm me.
> One day I'll jump
> out of my skin.
> I'll shake the sky
> like a hundred violins.

That's nice. That's very good, she said in her tired voice. You just remember to keep writing, Esperanza. You must keep writing. It will keep you free, and I said yes, but at that time I didn't know what she meant.[30]

The literature of new vision brings Chicanas full circle as it breaks through the source of our initial alienation from language: It breaks the bonds of religious and cultural oppression, not only using the word to press forward in the process of self-identification but at the same time providing an unappreciated form of self-representation of the "other" — the kind of self-representation experimental ethnographers are striving for. As indigenous ethnographers, Chicana creative writers provide readers with richly textured cultural critiques that negotiate the artificial boundaries created by traditional academic disciplines. Weaving aesthetic and social scientific interpretive methods, these writers surpass conventional feminist, literary, and anthropological readings with critiques that circumvent the traps hindering their approaches. They thus succeed in providing the kind of critical textual reading that leads to the self-awareness necessary for transformation. Film and cultural critic Teresa de Lauretis discusses the importance of this type of feminist interpretation, suggesting that these readings allow others to understand what it means to speak "as a woman." These critical readings instate awareness of the experiences and contradictions that surround the term *woman* in a way that transforms the textual representation into a performance that exceeds the text. "For women to enact the contradiction is to demonstrate the non-coincidence of woman as text, as image, is to resist identification with that image. It is to have stepped through the looking glass."[31]

I want to emphasize again that the four modes of Chicana literature I have outlined represent interdependent rather than sequential intervals. To consider the literature in a linear fashion would be to reduce it to a static text, negating its movement and performance qualities. The correlation and fluidity of the four modes, marked by a succession of strong and weak elements, depict opposite or different conditions that in turn make up the entire musical score. Some writers compose in all four intervals, while others limit themselves to one.

In Lydia Camarillo's "Mi Reflejo," we see how a single poem can include all four manners of expression: The work begins with the question "Who goes there?" and response "It is I." This question and response repeat throughout the poem, evoking the spirits and stories of women in Mexican history, as Camarillo reappropriates and reinscribes that history in female terms, alternating Spanish and English to develop a new discourse on *identidad*. She begins with The Conquest:

> Conquistaste y colonizaste mi gente.
> You alienated me from my people.
> Me hiciste la "Vendida".
> Ya no te acuerdas de me?
> I am Malinche.

Camarillo goes on to evoke Sor Juana Ines de la Cruz, Frida Kahlo, and la Virgen de Guadalupe in a chantlike rhythm. Progressing dialectically, the poem moves through the mode of rage and opposition, establishing Mexican women's history in a chronological sequence, setting the foundation for a point of view that has been either forgotten or suppressed. Camarillo closes this "poetic" cultural intervention by stating that women today are reflections of the past:

Si somos espejos de cada una,
Soy Malinche,
Soy la Virgen de Guadalupe,
Soy Sor Juana Ines de la Cruz,
Soy Frida Kahlo
Soy Mujer.[32]

"Mi Reflejo" draws from the four modes of expression I have outlined, though not in sequence. Reversing the final two modes, Camarillo's opening represents the new-vision phase in its suggestion that, as a social category, "woman" combines historical past and present. The poet concludes her colloquy in the mode of struggle and identification, stating that, as reflections of the past, women represent half of the struggle against oppression and asserting that, together with our *companeros,* "we are the Revolution."

Like a musical composition, Chicana literature resonates with a variety of themes or states of existence that provide the raw data for cultural interpretation. Chicana literary production supplies the voices, identifies the issues, and performs the rituals necessary for including women of color in the ongoing debate among mainstream feminist theorists. In the chapters that follow I build on the four modes of consciousness outlined here by considering how Chicana writers are engaged in an overall self-fashioning project that challenges and experiments with a variety of mainstream perceptions.

3

The House on Mango Street:
An Appropriation of Word,
Space, and Sign

In the Western social imagination the calendar year 1984 was marked for an examination of political power. George Orwell's 1949 masterpiece, *Nineteen Eighty-Four,* had forecast a bleak dystopian world characterized by state torture, thought police, and a culture of total paranoia — a world, in the words of the critic Fredric Jameson, where conspiracy had become social totality.[1] Aside from the wide range of commentary that attempted to take the measure of the culture's paranoia and progress, that year witnessed a revitalized interest in Chicana literature.

Although the National Association for Chicano Studies had organized annual conventions for eleven years, not until 1984 at the twelfth national conference in Austin, Texas, were scholars sanctioned by the theme of the convention — Voces de la Mujer — to address issues related to an emergent Chicana feminist movement. The high point of the conference featured a Chicana reading and book signing sponsored by Arte Publico Press to announce its new emphasis on women's literary production. Of the five books featured — Pat Mora's *Chants*; Evangelina Vigil's *Woman of Her Word: An Anthology of Writing by Latinas* and *Thirty an' Seen a Lot*; Ana Castillo's *Women Are Not Roses*; and Sandra Cisneros's *The House on Mango Street* — only Sandra Cisneros's *Mango Street* defied the poetic form previously privileged by many Chicana writers. In a text of forty-four poetically charged vignettes centering on women's experiences, Cisneros defined a distinctive Chicana literary space — oh so gently she flung down the gauntlet, challenging, at the least, accepted literary form, gender inequities, and the cultural and economic subordination of minorities. Theoretically speaking, this little text subverts traditional form and content in a way that demonstrates how conventional applications of literary genre and the social construction of gender undermine a "feminist aesthetic."[2]

Because *The House on Mango Street* is composed of short, independent, yet interrelated narratives, some critics have compared it to Tomás Rivera's *Y No Se Lo Tragó La Tierra*, consequently classifying it as a novel.[3] Although valid on some levels, the comparison points up the tendency to categorize women's literary production by measuring it against what has been deemed the universal (generally masculine) standard. Terry Eagleton has concluded that literary scholars, acting as custodians of a doctrine, work to preserve a particular discourse, defending it from other forms of debate, initiating newcomers, determining their level of mastery. Thus "certain pieces of writing are selected as being more amenable to this discourse than others, and these are what is known as literature or the 'literary canon.'"[4] In similar fashion, Chicano critical evaluations of *Mango Street* emphasize not its innovative approach, but rather its relationship to the Chicano literary canon. In Eagleton's terms, their primary objective has been to preserve Chicano discourse and acknowledge new writers who have successfully mastered convention. This kind of authorized control undermines exchange and fails to recognize that the social positioning of Chicana writers often compels them to respond to both European- and Mexican-influenced value systems.

The House on Mango Street breaks with the traditional bildungsroman even as it demonstrates how coming-of-age in a patriarchal society shapes a recognition of prescribed gender roles. The freedom and independence associated with male coming-of-age narratives has typically been replaced in the female versions by loss of freedom and acceptance of subordination; the narratives have tended to portray imprisoned, trapped, or isolated women. But *Mango Street*'s young heroine escapes isolation and succeeds on "male terms" as she experiences integration and freedom. The book's episodes challenge societal and cultural codes by emphasizing the protagonist's refusal to accept prescribed gender limitations. Classifying this work by means of a simplistic comparison to Rivera's standard rite-of-passage narrative, *Y No Se Lo Tragó La Tierra,* thus seems to me to depreciate Cisneros's experimental critique of gender inequality.

Mango Street also subverts conventional literary form, blurring genres and linking poetic vignettes to illustrate the day-to-day experiences and perceptions of Esperanza, an adolescent growing up in a Chicago barrio.[5] Cisneros calls the stories in *Mango Street* "lazy poems," the product of genre fusion. "For me each of the stories could've developed into poems, but they were not poems. They were stories, albeit hovering in that grey area between two genres. My newer work is still exploring this terrain."[6]

Cast as an ideological foil, *Mango*'s protagonist enables the author to shrewdly introduce a variety of political concerns that confront Chicano/a communities in the United States. Cisneros plays off a tension between the simplicity of the young narrator's point of view and the somber realities she represents, beginning with the title story, which opens the book.

> We didn't always live on Mango Street. Before that we lived on Loomis on the third floor, and before that we lived on Keeler. Before Keeler it was Paulina, and before that I can't remember. But what I remember most is moving a lot. . . . We had to leave the flat on Loomis quick. The water pipes broke and the landlord wouldn't fix them because the house was too old. We had to leave fast. We were using the washroom next door and carrying water over in empty milk gallons.[7]

Later through Esperanza's reflections, readers become privy to the individual alienation and shame created by her family's plight.

> I want a house on a hill like the ones with the gardens where Papa works. We go on Sundays, Papa's day off. I used to go. I don't anymore. You don't like to go out with us, Papa says. Getting too old? Getting too stuck-up says Nenny. I don't tell them I am ashamed—all of us staring out the window like the hungry. I am tired of looking at what we can't have. (M81)

On an ideological level, Esperanza dreams the American dream; on a material level, like all in her community she remains systematically excluded from it.

Even if the views of her protagonist are naive, Cisneros's depiction of Esperanza itself represents a refined challenge to domination. Cisneros's portrayal of the social predicament contributing to her protagonist's confusion is a symbolic act of resistance on the author's part.

What I am suggesting is that "serious" political inquiry should consider not only the oppositional tactics of the protagonist, but also the representation of the hegemonic system through which societal boundaries and the conditions for resistance are created. Rosaura Sánchez underscores the relationship of cultural boundaries to social, economic, and ideological limitations that are more tangible than ethnic or even national boundaries.

> If we consider acculturation at both ideological and material levels, ethnic groups in this country can be seen to suffer both inclusion and exclusion. Ideologically, thanks to the media and to our educational system, these groups will probably all have swallowed the same myths and yet, materially, be excluded from the lifestyle, goods and services that characterize the life of middle classes in the U.S.[8]

Cisneros's protagonist embodies the ideological and material acculturation Sánchez describes. Esperanza simultaneously experiences inclusion and exclusion.

The tension becomes more complex when we consider the points of view of author and narrator. The book's tendency to conflate the two perspectives has led some critics to argue that Esperanza's narrative (and, by implication, Cisneros's politics) simply illustrates an individual's desire for a house outside the barrio. This viewpoint fails to regard Cisneros's attempts to distinguish between Mexican cultural tradition and the social injustices Chicano communities have inherited. Therefore the implication is that an assimilationist point of view makes the text and the author problematic for social activists who associate the barrio with cultural pride.[9]

As do all rite-of-passage narratives, *Mango Street* represents maturation. Readers witness a subtle shift in the protagonist's understanding as she begins to consider some of the issues contributing to her subordinate cultural position. Yet despite this movement toward self-awareness and sophistication, Esperanza's voice holds echoes of some of her childish, impressionistic perceptions; consequently her visions of success and escape seem limited and naive. In "Geraldo No Last Name," for example, she has difficulty understanding why her friend Marin concerns herself about a hit-and-run victim, a young man she had met at a dance.

> But what difference does it make? He wasn't anything to her. He wasn't her boyfriend or anything like that. Just another *brazer* who didn't speak English. Just another wetback. You know the kind the ones who always look ashamed. (M 63)

If this is the level of Esperanza's maturation, the extent of her cultural awareness, what are readers to make of the author's point of view? Susan Lanser's study of narrative is instructional here; her conceptual model that distinguishes between the point of view of the "real author" and the "narrator" enables us to appreciate Cisneros's narrative quandary. As writer, Cisneros sends a text to her audience. This text combines an authorial voice with a collection of women's voices from the barrio that together create an image for the reader. These textual voices send a message to the readership. "Paradoxically, the structure of textual communicators is part of the message itself."[10] Lanser shows how the structure of textual voices functions to achieve authorial communication. To guide readers through *Mango Street,* as the "real author" Cisneros develops a discursive space that includes her dedication "a las mujeres," the ordering of the stories, and the use of narrative voices.

Cultural, Social, and Economic Boundaries

Through Esperanza, Cisneros shows readers how class boundaries and ideologies perpetuate a world that allows individuals to perform their social roles without considering the real conditions of their existence. Like other female members of poor ethnic communities, Esperanza suffers the inevitable consequences of race, class, and gender oppression. In her, the representative of a class of marginalized and subsequently alienated individuals, Cisneros shows "real" readers the limitations of an ideology that simply envisions liberation in individualistic terms. She advances her social critique by exposing a variety of barrio experiences.

In the fourth story, "My Name," it becomes clear that Esperanza wishes to reinvent herself in order to transcend the limitations that result from her ethnic identity. Throughout *Mango Street* she has seemed to feel more embarrassed than angry about her situation; now we hear her innermost thoughts about self-fashioning.

In English my name means hope. In Spanish it means too many letters. It means sadness, it means waiting. It is like the number nine. A muddy color. It is the Mexican records my father plays on Sunday mornings. When he is shaving, songs like sobbing. It was my great-grandmother's name and now it is mine. She was a horse woman too, born like me in the Chinese year of the horse — but I think this is a Chinese lie because the Chinese, like the Mexicans, don't like their women strong. . . . I would like to baptize myself under a new name, a name more like the real me, the one nobody sees. Esperanza as Lizandra or Maritza or Zeze the X. Yes. Something like Zeze the X will do. (M12)

In this story as in other Chicana literature, "grandmother" signifies the symbolic matriarchal handing down of cultural traditions.[11] But Cisneros's Esperanza subverts the usual process, stating, "I have inherited her name, but I don't want to inherit her place by the window." Overturning the customary nostalgic sentiment that associates grandmothers with positive cultural nourishment, Cisneros's great-grandmother represents "traditional, cultural values" as confining and debilitating. Thus Esperanza wants a culturally uncoded new name — Zeze the X.[12]

By providing a critique of the "traditional" Mexican female experience, Cisneros's stories serve as an ethnographic allegory of female humanity, for they "simultaneously describe real cultural events and make additional moral, ideological, and even cosmological statements."[13] Through the words of her young protagonist, Cisneros has made a precarious start on a project of cultural critique. Adrienne Rich calls this kind of writing "Revision — the act of looking back, of seeing with fresh eyes, of entering an old text from a new critical direction." It is, Rich says, "for women more than a chapter in cultural history: it is an act of survival. Until we understand the assumptions in which we are drenched we cannot know ourselves." Rich argues that women cannot reenvision themselves without first having a clear understanding of the past; and they must know it differently than they have ever known it, in order not to pass on a tradition but to break its hold over them. "Thus, a feminist rewriting of literature would begin first by examining how women have been living, how they have been led to imagine themselves, how the very act of naming has been till now a male prerogative."[14]

Since Esperanza's reflections in "My Name" begin by considering the cultural implications of naming itself, what seems to reflect an internally oppressive state à la Paulo Freire can, if we are influenced by Rich's thinking, instead be viewed as a healthy step toward self-actualization. Cisneros illustrates how Esperanza's name, which in "English . . . means hope," is quickly distorted to mean a "sadness and waiting," a dramatic shift in meaning predicated on gender, culture, and class oppression. Readers here witness an ideological shift that transforms the noun *esperanza* (hope) into the verb *esperar* (to wait); we see that Esperanza's most personal experiences are determined by outside forces. Esperanza does not control her own destiny; she is a passive agent acted upon by a system beyond her control.

A story of a Chicana caught between two cultural systems, "My Name" is also an allegory of the powerless role of the colonized individual, thrown into high relief by Esperanza's naive point of view. As James Clifford has shown, "allegory prompts us to say of any cultural description not 'this represents, or symbolizes, that' but rather, 'this is a (morally charged) story about that.'"[15] To fully understand the motivation behind the narrative approach of this "real author," consider Freire's analysis of the colonization process.

For cultural invasion to succeed, it is essential that those invaded become convinced of their intrinsic inferiority. Since everything has its opposite, if those who are invaded consider themselves inferior, they must necessarily recognize the superiority of the invaders. . . . The more invasion is accentuated and those invaded are alienated from the spirit of their own culture and from themselves, the more the latter want to be like the invaders: to walk like them, dress like them, talk like them.[16]

Mango Street depicts Esperanza's internalized oppression, a state of mind prompted by her belief in the American dream and her desire for the escape that assimilation offers. In "Alicia and I Talking on Edna's Steps," Alicia, recognizing Esperanza's self-contempt, counsels her to remember who she is and where she came from.

You live right here, 4006 Mango, Alicia says and points to the house I am ashamed of. No, this isn't my house I say and shake my head as if shaking could undo the year I've lived here. I don't belong. I don't ever want to come from here. You have a home, Alicia, and one day you'll go there, to a little town you remember, but me I never had a house, not even a photograph . . . only one I dream of. No, Alicia says. Like it or not you are Mango Street and one day you'll come back too. Not me. Not until somebody makes it better. (M 99)

Esperanza, frustrated because her desires and her material reality seem inconsistent, reconciles her feelings by expressing shame and discontent.

The House as Symbol

Franz Fanon has outlined three stages that characterize the works of native writers who challenge colonial structures. In the first phase, "a period of unqualified assimilation," the native writer gives proof that she has assimilated the occupying power. In the second, the native writer is disturbed; "he decides to remember what he is. . . . Past happenings of the bygone days of his childhood will be brought up out of the depths of his memory; old legends will be reinterpreted in the light of a borrowed aestheticism and of a conception of the world which was discovered under other skies." Although often symptomatic of a period of distress and difficulty characterized by experiences of death and disgust, the literature of this phase is dominated by humor and allegory. (In stage three, the writer reveals a clear sense of political autonomy.)[17]

Firmly planted in Fanon's second phase, Cisneros uses her protagonist to subtly equate the assimilated mind-set with that of a naive adolescent. Her narrative strategy gives her the freedom, in the final stories, to deconstruct childish, yet mainstream, assumptions. Now we witness a change in Esperanza's attitude. She begins to develop a critical awareness of social boundaries as she modifies her cultural perspective. In "Bums in the Attic," she states:

People who live on hills sleep so close to the stars they forget those of us who live too much on earth. They don't look down at all except to be content to live on hills. They have nothing to do with last week's garbage or fear of rats. Night comes. Nothing wakes them but the wind. One day I'll own my own house, but I won't forget who I am or where I came from. Passing bums will ask, Can I come in?

I'll offer them the attic, ask them to stay, because I know
how it is to be without a house. (M 81)

While Esperanza's reflections reveal limited social awareness, they
disclose the critical sophistication and literary skill of the "real
author." Through Esperanza's characterization, Cisneros depicts
some of the inner conflicts that develop as marginalized individuals
attempt to resolve the apparent disjunction between their desires
for cultural integrity and for individual liberation.

The symbol Cisneros chooses to represent the ideological, cultural, and economic limits imposed on the marginalized woman's
space is the house. For Esperanza, life becomes a struggle to secure
individual success and, her ultimate aspiration, a house of her own,
a home unlike her family's, which is "small and red with tight little
steps in front and windows so small you'd think they were holding
their breath. Bricks are crumbling in places, and the front door is so
swollen you have to push hard to get in" (M 8). Esperanza longs for
a house like the one in her mother's bedtime stories, "white with
trees around it, a great big yard and grass growing without a fence"
(M 8).

The narrative unfolds around this recurrent motif, introduced
in its title. *The House on Mango Street* subtly suggests a series of
possible readings. Even though the use of more than one language
in a single phrase is common in the United States, it nonetheless
represents a linguistic practice that accommodates diversity. Because Cisneros's title draws on two languages, it suggests a pri-
mordial blending of two cultural systems.[18] When we also consider how the concept of house lends itself to public and private
worlds, we are in a position to understand the breadth of Cisneros's narrative.

On a material level one's house symbolically reflects one's success and achievement to the outside world. Yet in more figurative terms, the word denotes the domestic sphere, a metonomy for women's space. To the private/public dialectic Cisneros adds yet another opposition: insider/outsider cultural values, the political implications of the dominant cultural system of the United States as well as the internal convictions emphasized by Mexican culture. House becomes the metaphor for success and escape from the limitations imposed on Chicanas by cultural traditions, as well as for the boundaries and limitations of poverty. The story "A House of My Own" underscores as it expands the issues raised by Virgina Woolf in *A Room of One's Own*:

> Not a flat. Not an apartment in back. Not a man's house. Not a daddy's. A house all my own. With my porch and my pillow, my pretty purple petunias. My books and my stories. My two shoes waiting beside the bed. Nobody to shake a stick at. Nobody's garbage to pick up after. Only a house quiet as snow, a space for myself to go, clean as paper before the poem. (M 100)

Cisneros's poetic text defies prosaic convention; syncopated fragments punctuated as complete thoughts make us aware of the writer's experimentation with form. "A House of My Own" graphically redefines domestic spaces as effectively as it crosses genres.

Writing as Revision

By taking her writing one step beyond the conventional, Cisneros has moved into a terrain explored by few Chicana writers. *The*

House on Mango Street not only exemplifies an act of revision that looks back with fresh eyes at the cultural history and day-to-day experiences of her young protagonist, Esperanza, it also redefines literary form in its mediation between the romantic and the harsh. In a later essay entitled "Ghosts and Voices," Cisneros recalls an experience in graduate school that inspired her text:

> During a seminar titled "On Memory and the Imagina-tion" when the class was heatedly discussing Gustav Bach-elard's Poetics of Space and the metaphor of a house — a house, a house, it hit me. What did I know except third-floor flats. Surely my classmates knew nothing about that. That's precisely what I chose to write; about third-floor flats, and fear of rats, and drunk husbands sending rocks through windows, anything as far from the poetic as pos-sible.[19]

Cisneros defies tradition by writing about censored topics and in the process demonstrates Adrienne Rich's point about wom-en's writing. Cisneros revises history by honestly confronting her past. She has embraced an assertive role, sculpting cultural impres-sions that have helped refine Chicana feminist aesthetics. Many of her vignettes dwell on the mundane and unromantic activities of women. "There Was an Old Woman She Had So Many Children She Didn't Know What to Do" inscribes the simple life of a single mother:

> Rosa Vargas' kids are too many and too much. It's not her fault you know, except she is their mother and only one against so many. They are bad those Vargas, and how can they help it with only one mother who is tired all the time

from buttoning and bottling and babying, and who cries every day for the man who left without even leaving a dollar for bologna or a note explaining how come. (M 30)

Cisneros's sophisticated critique of patriarchal control employs the simple language of an adolescent coming to terms with female dailiness in her community and constructs the foundation for a counterdiscourse. Her literary project is similar to historian Bettina Aptheker's. Confronting the absence of women in traditional historical accounts, Aptheker sets out to develop alternative approaches to conventional historiography, among them an examination of women's everyday experiences.

> By the dailiness of women's lives I mean the patterns women create and the meanings women invent each day and over time as a result of their labors, and in the context of their subordinated status to men. . . . The point is to suggest a way of knowing from the meanings women give to their labors.[20]

Both Aptheker and Cisneros are engaged in discursive projects that bring women from the margins to the center, recognizing them as active participants in history rather than pawns struggling for self-expression and escape.

Cisneros portrays the options available to women by presenting both positive and negative female role models and constructs a mosaic of common problems to convey not only women's struggles but also their tactics for conflict resolution. Mexican cultural practices maintain a system that classifies women according to their marital status; one is viewed either as a *senorita* (virgin) or as a *senora* (sexually active wife), a polarity that constantly forces women to define themselves as accessories to men.[21] A woman who steps outside these acceptable roles finds herself classified according to a masculine interpretation of history, she is viewed as a *puta*, that is as a harlot or sexual deviant.

Mango Street reflexively considers the ramifications of "heterosexist" ideologies through Cisneros's characterizations, which demonstrate how the feminine preoccupation with beauty, marriage, and regret is a product of patriarchal socialization. In the story "Sally," Cisneros alludes to male desire and the objectification of women.

> Sally is the girl with eyes like Egypt and nylons the color of smoke. The boys at school think she's beautiful because her hair is shiny black like raven feathers and when she laughs she flicks her hair back like a satin shawl over her shoulders and laughs. Her father says to be this beautiful is trouble. They are very strict in his religion. They are not supposed to dance. He remembers his sisters and he is sad. Then she can't go out. Sally I mean. (M 77)

This depiction illuminates the contradictions in an ideology whose primary objective is masculine gratification. The media's representational practices seduce women into thinking that their very existence depends on how successfully they prepare themselves for the male gaze. Sally's dilemma is that what enhances her attractiveness to "the boys" arouses her father's disapproval and concern; her placement between her father's expectations and the boys' desire renders her powerless. Women are caught in the double bind created by masculine anticipation and experience; recognizing their confinement in this gender-determined space, they develop the desire for freedom and self-control.

In the title character in "Marin," Esperanza's Puerto Rican friend, Cisneros depicts a conventional female strategy based solidly in a dominant (male) ideology. Accepting her inferior and powerless position as a woman in a man's world, Marin dreams of escaping from poverty.

> Marin says that if she stays here next year, she is going to get a real job downtown because that's where the best jobs are, since you always get to look beautiful and get to wear nice clothes and can meet someone in the subway who might marry and take you to live in a big house far away. (M 27)

Marin's strategy seems unsophisticated, especially when viewed ahistorically. Yet Cisneros's portrayal of Puerto Rico reaches beyond the experiences of minority women both in the United States to encompass the impact of all kinds of colonization on the female psyche. Marin's story moves us from the understanding of internal colonization we gained through Esperanza (the U.S.-born ethnic minority's tendency to seek acceptance through assimilation) to a comparison of internal and external colonization.

Because Marin is both a native of Puerto Rico and a woman, her tactics for advancement combine the influences of both identities. Cisneros's portrayal of her suggests a parallel between the aspirations of a woman who has accepted a subordinate position based on gender inequality and those of a colonized subject. Even as a U.S. colony, Puerto Rico continues to use Spanish as its official language. Consequently Puerto Ricans born in Puerto Rico have remained culturally semiautonomous. However, because of its sta-

tus of Free Associated State, Puerto Rico remains socially and eco-
nomically dependent on the United States. This colonial situation
obviously contributes to feelings of inferiority and insecurity for
the indigenous population, which lead individuals to negate their
native cultural influences in order to advance in the colonizer's
system. Franz Fanon argues that in such circumstances "every
effort is made to bring the colonized person to admit the inferiority
of his culture which has been transformed into instinctive patterns
of behavior, to recognize the unreality of his [nation], and, in the
last extreme, the confused and imperfect character of his own bio-
logical structure."[22]

In one short passage in the next story, "Alicia Who Sees Mice,"
Cisneros does not merely describe the limitations of patriarchal
systems but writes about the tension between the past and the
future, posing a solution that could enable women to transcend a
cultural legacy of "lunchbox tortillas" and "a woman's place."

> Close your eyes and they'll go away her father says, or
> you're just imagining. And anyway, a woman's place is
> sleeping so she can wake up early with the tortilla star. . . .
> Alicia, whose mama died, is sorry there is no one older to
> rise and make the lunchbox tortillas. Alicia, who inherited
> her mama's rolling pin and sleepiness, is young and smart
> and studies for the first time at the university. Two trains
> and a bus, because she doesn't want to spend her whole
> life in a factory or behind a rolling pin. (M32)

Here Cisneros sets up a counterdiscourse by articulating the protagonist's cultural critique within her feminist aesthetic. At this
moment the points of view of author and protagonist seem to
intersect, resisting dualistic thinking and dominant norms that re-

flect a masculinist way of seeing. Cisneros is thus engaged in a deconstructive process that divulges how what we think of as universalities or dominant traditions are often really no more than incomplete, gender-coded modes of perception.

In Esperanza's mother in "A Smart Cookie" Cisneros constructs her most stinging critique of the limitations that marriage places on women.

> I could've been somebody, you know? my mother says and sighs. She has lived in this city her whole life. She can speak two languages. She can sing an opera. She knows how to fix a T.V. But she doesn't know which subway train to take to get downtown. . . . Shame is a bad thing, you know. [Esperanza's mother continues]. It keeps you down. You want to know why I quit school? Because I didn't have nice clothes. No clothes, but I had brains. Yup, she says disgusted, stirring again. I was a smart cookie then. (M83)

Through this woman in conflict with her male-defined place in society, the story speaks of any woman's unfulfilled life, of her need to conform to the dictates of the patriarchy, to sacrifice herself to survive. Esperanza's mother, like many of the female characters Cisneros portrays, tragically enacts a sacrificial relationship of *separation* and *difference*.

Polite Indignation

Combining the author's insight with her protagonist's naiveté, the complex point of view of *Mango Street* addresses a multiplicity of spectators. Its tone, free of anger or accusation, on the surface innocent and dispassionate, allows Anglo American male and female readers to approach the text with relative ease; in this sense it differs from contemporary literature written by women of color. Adrienne Rich's critique of Virginia Woolf's voice in *A Room of One's Own* seems to apply equally to Cisneros's authorial voice in *The House on Mango Street*:

> It is a tone of a woman almost in touch with her anger, who is determined not to appear angry, who is willing herself to be calm, detached, and even charming in a roomful of men where things have been said which are attacks on her very integrity. Virginia Woolf is addressing an audience of women, but she is acutely conscious — as she always was — of being overheard by men. . . . She drew the language out into an exacerbated thread in her determination to have her own sensibility yet protect it from those masculine presences. Only at rare moments in that essay do you hear the passion in her voice; she was trying to sound as cool as Jane Austen, as Olympian as Shakespeare, because that is the way the men of the culture thought a writer should sound.[23]

Rich's description enables us to see why *Mango Street,* like Woolf's *A Room of One's Own,* has been applauded by mainstream feminists and at the same time regarded as too assimilationist by some Chicano/a critics.

Because *Mango Street* can be read from a variety of non-threatening positions, it has been used in many universities as a primer for raising consciousness about gender oppression; it seems to challenge patriarchal institutions and cultures gently, from an apparently middle-class, mainstream perspective. Closer reading, however, reveals the voice of innocence and naiveté as a narrative strategy that allows the author to construct a safe space from which, paradoxically, she can expose the existential estrangement that derives from cultural and economic subordination. The narrative thus functions as the ultimate strategy for escape from confining traditions. Cisneros enables her readers to look critically at the assumptions that engulf them.

4

Shades of the Indigenous Ethnographer: Ana Castillo's *Mixquiahuala Letters*

Sandra Cisneros uses fiction as a medium for social commentary. Like that of many other Chicana creative writers, her work contributes to an emergent literary tradition that emphasizes cultural traditions and in this respect resembles the writing produced by contemporary cultural anthropologists. To my mind, the overwhelming similarities between ethnography and Chicana creative writing suggest that we have reached a point in our social development wherein new levels of awareness and sensitivity about issues of "difference" directly affect all forms of representation. Because a desire for authenticity motivates the writers of both ethnographic and Chicana creative-writing projects, they share the narrative problems that arise with attempts to "accurately" portray culture.

Focusing on these similarities, in this chapter I introduce an interpretive method that integrates contemporary textual anthropology and Chicana cultural production. For example, both begin with the selection of a story deemed worthy of representation. In this process of feminist intervention, the similarities are readily apparent.[1] Here I treat Ana Castillo's *Mixquiahuala Letters* as an indigenous ethnography that, like Marjorie Shostak's feminist ethnography, blends personal narrative with cultural analysis; I also argue that Castillo's text can be read as parody of the classical ethnographic practice, wherein:

> the anthropologist closely observes, records, and engages in the daily life of another culture — an experience labeled as the fieldwork method — and then writes accounts of this culture, emphasizing descriptive detail. These accounts are the primary form in which fieldwork procedures, the other culture, and the ethnographer's personal and theoretical reflections are accessible to professionals and other readerships.[2]

Throughout the chapter I compare and interweave Castillo's text with Marjorie Shostak's self-reflexive ethnography *Nisa: The Life and Words of a Kung Woman,* which exemplifies a new trend in feminist anthropology and illustrates beautifully the relationship between feminist ethnographic methods and Castillo's creative process.

Feminist Ethnography: *Nisa*

Shostak begins her cultural exploration by explaining to potential informants what she is interested in hearing about:

Memories of childhood; feelings about parents, siblings, relatives, and friends; adolescence and experiences with other children; dreams; marriage; the birth of children; childhood sex and adult sex; relationships with husbands and lovers; feelings about death; thoughts about the future; and anything else they felt was important in their lives. I made it clear that everything would be confidential as long as I was there and if and when I returned to the region. I told them I would, however, share the material with people in my own country, so that they could learn about Kung women's lives.[3]

With this passage we witness Shostak's meta-editorial process at work as we become privy to the way her informants are made aware of the marketability of women's narratives.

The ethnographer's role as cultural producer becomes more apparent as Shostak describes her process of selecting informants and her discovery of Nisa's gift for storytelling.

Among the women I interviewed, Nisa stood out. She had an exceptional ability to tell a story in a way that was generous, vibrant, and moving. Her sensitivity and skill made her stories larger and more important than the details they comprised. Sometimes they captured the most subtle and profound experiences in human life; sometimes they revealed a confused human entanglement that was all too recognizable. This was the value that her narrative had formed, and the reason it became so compelling. . . . Most of her stories were described in rich detail and told with a beginning, a middle, and an end. If I questioned her before she had finished, she often said, "Wait. I'm getting to that. Now, listen." (Nisa 40)

Unlike conventional ethnographers, Shostak meticulously outlines her fieldwork method; in this process we can draw the parallels between ethnography and ethnic-American literary production. Like other feminist ethnographies, *Nisa* is conceived and orchestrated by an authority who controls the means of production, an anthropologist who openly reveals that she is in pursuit of narratives that represent real events in the realm of women's experiences. In the same way, Chicana writers, prompted by their desire to depict alternative cultural perspectives that address women's concerns, compose texts that are sustained by feminist interest and their subsequent marketability.

Further, the feminist anthropologist and the Chicana creative writer both use subjective narration to portray "authentic" yet distinct realities. Hayden White reminds us that the value cultural critics have "attached to narrativity in the representation of real events arises out of a desire to have real events display the coherence, integrity, fullness, and closure of an image of life that is and can only be imaginary. The notion that sequences of real events possess the formal attributes of the stories we tell about imaginary events could only have its origin in wishes, daydreams, reveries."[4] Shostak's reflections on the accuracy of one of her informant's stories suggest that she is cognizant of the narrative limitations to which White alludes.

Not knowing the answers, I only hoped that Bau hadn't been lying. I tried to assess how likely that was, considering all I knew about her. She was quiet and reserved and did not constantly seek me out. Only after weeks of talking together had she started to confide in me. . . . All in all, I felt quite certain that she had told me what she believed to be true. If so, then, whatever her personal biases, I now had a base from which to explore further. Naturally, I would ask other people similar questions in order to determine the overall validity of Bau's confidences, but she had given me something to go on. (Nisa 43)

Because Shostak understands the limits as well as the value of narrative she suggests that her ethnography, which focuses on the life and experiences of a single Kung woman, should not be interpreted as anything other than a singular cultural representation.

Nisa's narrative is just one view of Kung life. Her history does not represent the whole range of experience available to women in her culture; the life stories of other women are often quite different. Also, it is not possible to take everything Nisa says literally, particularly her descriptions of her earlier years. She enjoyed the interview situation with the "machine that grabs your voice." To make her story lively and dramatic, she often assumed the high somewhat insistent voice of a young child as though trying to describe the events of her childhood through the eyes of Nisa, the little girl. (Nisa 43)

Shostak is aware of her role as feminist anthropologist and the influence and limitations it imposes on Nisa's narrative. In order to remedy this situation, she makes a proposal that her fieldwork account be thought of as a subjective cultural interpretation, for, as Hayden White suggests, "narrative in general from the folktale to the novel, from the annals to the fully realized 'history,' has to do with the topics of law, legality, legitimacy, or, more generally, authority."[5]

Chicana Meta-ethnography

The correlation I make between Chicana creative expression and feminist ethnography is based largely on the assumption that narrative mediates between what is real and what is imagined, taking into account problems of authority and legitimacy. A textual analysis of Ana Castillo's *Mixquiahuala Letters* will help illuminate this idea.

The novel is a postmodernist, Chicana feminist work that reflects the historical forces of the eighties, as well as diverse literary and other concerns recognized and legitimized by the American literary canon.[6] Through detailed descriptions, Castillo presents an oppositional perspective that confronts the inherent restrictions imposed on women by both Anglo American and Mexican culture.

Because Chicano tradition draws on at least two origins — the longstanding culture one is born into and the culture of social and political forces in one's immediate environment — anthropologists have categorized it as a "creole culture." As I have argued, such notions disregard the influence of gender and thus fail to recognize that Chicana writers must mediate and negotiate between two patriarchal systems if they wish to construct an autonomous cultural and feminist identity. As a bold cultural intervention, Chicana literature thus resembles what we have come to respect as interpretive ethnography.

Consider Clifford Geertz's 1973 statement that "there is no such thing as human nature independent of culture" juxtaposed with one from Ana Castillo in 1986: "There was a definite call to find a place to satisfy my yearning spirit, the Indian in me that had begun to cure the ails of humble folk distrustful of modern medicine; a need for the sapling woman for the fertile earth that nurtured her growth." Using different discursive practices and addressing different audiences, Geertz and Castillo raise related issues. In his elaborate discussion of culture in *The Interpretation of Cultures,* Geertz contends that humans are like animals suspended in "webs of significance" they themselves have spun. Analyzing these webs should be viewed not as an experimental scientific search for law but rather as an interpretative search for meaning. If humans are suspended in cultural webs, it follows that there can be "no such thing as human nature independent of culture."[7] Taken out of their anthropological context, Geertz's ideas seem innocent enough, but we must remember that as an ethnographer he is speaking in terms of "the Other" and of "primitive culture." If we avoid the subtle trappings of this hegemonic perspective, we can apply his metaphor to the self-fashioning process racialized ethnic groups in the United States undertake as they attempt to create an existence that draws from two distinct cultural systems. (Interestingly, Geertz's interpretive mode of cultural analysis — "thick description," he calls it — has been employed by many feminist scholars involved in decoding and interpreting women's culture.)

In contrast to Geertz's, Castillo's words appear in a work of fiction, *The Mixquiahuala Letters.* She makes no claims of fact but states in the introduction that "any resemblance" her book "may have to actual persons or incidents is coincidental." Nevertheless the quotation reveals the similarity of her text to Geertz's factual account: Both grapple with the influence of an elusive but powerful cultural force.

Castillo's readers soon become aware that her protagonist's well-being depends on culture. And when we carry forward Geertz's semiotic concept of culture and evaluate the ethnographic writings of traditional anthropologists as representations based on individual interpretations, it becomes difficult to identify them as objective, factual accounts of reality. Consequently, once we recognize that these cultural inscriptions represent a mixture of descriptive and interpretive modes of discourse, the gap between fiction and ethnography shrinks. Both forms of writing are distilled into a particular way of seeing; both Castillo and Geertz are involved in projects that aspire to describe and interpret culture.

Apart from a somewhat natural affinity, the two quotations also illustrate the vast difference between objective and subjective writing. In the assertive language of an "authority," Geertz states that all human nature is influenced by culture. Castillo's more reflective language embroiders upon and brings to life Geertz's academic yet direct observation; her words illustrate why or how his thoughts might apply to the real world of subjective experiences. In juxtaposition, both insights seem to expand. Castillo's fiction grounds Geertz's theory in practice—a particularly useful strategy when applied to the Chicana (feminist) writer's quest for self-definition.

Marginality and Self-Fashioning

As I have shown, fashioning a marginal identity (Chicana, feminist, or hyphenated American) requires a series of negotiations and mediations between the past and the future. For the Chicana, this past and future are culturally explosive territories in terms of women's experiences and historical implications, because today she must attempt to define herself as she maneuvers between opposing realities that both fail to acknowledge her existence: the Chicano and the Anglo-feminist. The nostalgic Chicano plan of the past idealizes old customs — patriarchal interpretations of Mexican cultural traditions and history. Its partiality is augmented by an Anglo-feminist plan that either confines Chicanas to debilitating cultural stereotypes or envisions a future that has for the most part failed to acknowledge female difference based on class and ethnicity.

Ana Castillo's *Mixquiahuala Letters* portrays two Chicanas caught between these polarities, moving closer to self-discovery by synthesizing aspects from both Anglo and Mexican cultures, weaving a complicated present out of the past and future options. Teresa and Alicia are friends who share experiences traveling and living in Mexico and the United States. In the daily activities of these women, Castillo exposes some of the problems that arise whenever an individual judged nonessential attempts to fashion an identity that rebuts that very dominant perception that has served to marginalize her.

Although Stephen Greenblatt's *Renaissance Self-Fashioning* focuses on the literature of the Renaissance, his distinctions between self-identification in the upper and in the marginal classes make his approach valuable to this inquiry. He states that, for marginal classes,

> self-fashioning is achieved in relation to something perceived as alien, strange, or hostile . . . self-fashioning al-

ways involves some experience of threat, some effacement or undermining, some loss of self . . . and may say that self-fashioning occurs at the point of encounter between an authority and an alien, that what is produced in this encounter partakes of both the authority and the alien that is marked for attack, and hence that way achieved identity always contains within itself the signs of its own subversion or loss.[8]

In light of Greenblatt's analysis, we can see how the Chicanas' self-fashioning "always involves some experience of threat" or "some loss of self." Castillo's protagonist, Teresa, speaks of such a loss when she reflects on her relationship to Mexico in Letter nineteen:

> Mexico. Melancholy, profoundly right and wrong, it embraces as it strangulates.
>
> Destiny is not a metaphysical confrontation with one's self rather, society has knit its pattern so tight that a confrontation with it is inevitable. (ML 59)

Her words reflect a deep understanding of what she perceives to be a Mexican woman's destiny, determined not through confronting one's self, but rather through confronting a society that can restrict, silence, and marginalize women.

In "Letter Thirteen" to Alicia, Teresa reveals her attitudes toward another threat, Anglo women.

> why i hated white women and sometimes didn't like you: Society had made them above all possessions the most desired. And they believed it. My husband admitted feel-

ing inferior to them. . . . i hated white women who took black pimps everyone knows savages have bestial members i hated white women who preferred Latins and Mediterraneans because of the fusion of hot and cold blood running through the very core of their erections and nineteenth-century romanticism that makes going to bed with them much more challenging than with WASP men who are only good for making money and marrying. (ML 43)

As a symbolic representation of cultural attitudes, this letter tells us something basic about the Chicana woman's experience. Yet Teresa's report that her husband felt inferior to white women illustrates that the threat they pose moves beyond gender distinctions.

With this letter Castillo unmasks one of the ideological limitations of Anglo American feminist theory, its lack of concern for issues of ethnicity, class, or culture. When white women are elevated to the status of "most desired," Teresa's letter suggests, the subordination and control of women of color intensifies in the backlash, because the standard for beauty is based on light skin. This inferior position, which reflects the way men objectify women, complements the subaltern status Anglo American feminist theorists relegate to women of color. Through cultural production, Chicana writers can critique the systems that oppress them and thereby begin to establish autonomy.

Greenblatt deems autonomy important but not the central issue, which is one's power to impose a shape upon oneself, to control one's identity. And the interplay between external forces, which encompass time and space as well as past and future, is what determines this self-fashioning, according to Greenblatt, Clifford

Geertz, and for that matter many Chicano writers. One way to consider these "external forces" and their implications for Chicanas attempting to define themselves in cultural and feminist terms is to focus on how Castillo's *Mixquiahuala Letters* negotiates between them.

Chicana critic Norma Alarcón conceives of Chicana poets as "umpires" mediating between a patriarchal interpretation of the past that relegates women to "crippling traditional stereotypes" and the equally limiting future depicted in the "Anglo American feminist promise."[9] In *The Mixquiahuala Letters,* Ana Castillo has shifted from poet "umpire" to feminist ethnographer by producing a personal narrative that falls between objective (real) and subjective narratives (imagined), thereby overcoming what James Clifford has called anthropology's "impossible attempt to fuse objective and subjective practices."[10]

To view *The Mixquiahuala Letters* as such a personal narrative is to examine the social sciences and literature together, to set new parameters that can accommodate more comprehensive theorizing. The implementation of an interdisciplinary method not only transforms anthropology's impossibilities into probabilities but also transcends fictive (imagined) form. Once we make this leap in consciousness, opening rather than closing our respective discourses, limitations and fragmented concepts begin to dissipate.

Ethnographic Parody

Because Castillo's novel consists of letters that systemically observe, record, and describe daily Mexican and American experiences — the same processes used in fieldwork — we can read it as a serious parody of modern ethnographic and travel writing. Linda Hutcheon in *A Theory of Parody* draws upon the double etymology of the prefix *para-* to conclude that "on a pragmatic level parody was not limited to producing a ridiculous effect [*para-* as counter or against], but that the equally strong suggestion of complicity and accord [*para-* as 'beside'] allowed for an opening up of the range of parody." This distinction has been used to argue for the existence of serious as well as comedic parody.[11]

As a serious parody of modern ethnography, Castillo's text records the voices and experiences involved in growing up Chicana. Like fieldwork, it reveals "unsuspected connections among sets of social activities and cultural forms."[12] And like an ethnographer, Castillo uses the voice of her informant, Teresa, to focus on what is at risk when a Chicana attempts to fashion an identity that conforms to two opposing cultures. She subverts the epistolary form the way that Marjorie Shostak experiments with ethnographic writing; both use their narratives to freely associate between issues and cultures as they describe the effects of patriarchal institutions and beliefs on the relationship between the sexes.

In "Letter Four," Teresa foregrounds the way the Catholic church molds individual Mexican/Chicana identity into a cultural model that promotes women's passivity and guilt.

Alicia,

Do you know the *smell* of a church? Not a storefront, praise the Lord, hallelujah church, or a modest frame building with a simple steeple projecting to the all heavens, but a CATHEDRAL, with doors the height of two very tall men and so heavy that when you pull one open to enter you feel as small as you are destined.

You were never led by the hand as a little girl by a godmother, or tugged by the ear by a nun whose dogmatic instruction initiated you into humility which is quite different from baptism when you were anointed with water as a squirming baby in the event that you should die and never see God face-to-face because you had not been cleansed of the sin of your parents' copulation.

It smells of incense, hot oils, the wax of constant burning candles, melting at a vigilant pace, the plaster of an army of saints watching with fixed glass eyes, revered in exchange for being mediators and delivering your feeble prayers. It smells of flowers and palms that precede Easter. It smells of death.

The last time i went to CHURCH, genuflecting my way to the confessional, i was eighteen years old.

i was a virgin, technically speaking, a decent girl, having been conditioned to put my self-respect before curiosity. This did not satisfy the priest, or should i say, stimulate his stagnant duty in that dark closet of anonymity and appointed judgement.

He began to probe. When that got him no titillating results, he suggested, or more precisely, led an interrogation founded on gestapo technique. When i didn't waiver under the torment, although feeling my knees raw, air spare, he accused outright: "*Are you going to tell me you haven't wanted to be with a man? You must have let one do more than . . . than what?*

i ran out of the booth in tears and in a rage, left the CHURCH without waiting to hear my penance for absolution of my unforgivable sins. (ML 24–25, emphasis in the original)

Teresa's narrative describes as it critiques the religious institution responsible for the indoctrination and ensuing violation of women's consciousness. At eighteen, Teresa suffers an emotional violation, the penetrating imagination of the priest in the confessional.

It is interesting to compare Castillo's literary discussion with Majorie Shostak's ethnographic exploration of women and sexuality in Kung culture. Shostak's chapter "Discovering Sex" includes Nisa's account of her first experience with sex:

> Once Tikay tore off my pubic apron and threw it up in a tree where it just stayed, hanging. He wanted to have sex with me, but I didn't want to. He grabbed me and I fought with him; he grabbed my chest and grabbed all over my body. Even though I still had no breasts, he kept grabbing and holding on to me. I said, "Are my genitals supposed to be having sex? No, I haven't even started to develop yet. You're the one with the penis, but me, I have no genitals to have sex with. Because just as you have a penis, I don't have a vagina! When God made your penis and put it there, God didn't make a vagina to put there for me. I have no vagina at all. My genital area is bare. So how can you have sex with something that's not there?" He said, "I'll have sex with you!" . . . I refused and started to cry. That's when he tore off my pubic apron and threw it up in a tree. I shouted, "I don't care! Feel bad! You won't have sex with me!" I stood there crying, covering my genitals with my hands because there was nothing else covering me. (Nisa 119–20)

Like Teresa's, Nisa's narrative emphasizes female inexperience and subsequent shame brought about by a sexually explicit male agenda that objectifies women. The priest responds to Teresa with his preconceived fantasies and assumptions about women. Even as children, Tikay and Nisa seem as aware of the power that comes with the phallus as they are of the limitations and powerlessness attributed to women. (Their male/female interaction undermines Shostak's introductory discussion, which frames the chapter within the context of sexuality and Kung children's play habits.) Patriarchal beliefs and expectations leave Nisa crying and covering her genitals and Teresa running from the "CHURCH" in tears and rage.

The reflex form of the epistolary novel gives Castillo the flexibility to compare and contrast the way women are viewed in the United States and Mexico. In an entry devoted to recollections about her experiences in Veracruz, Teresa recalls a conversation with Ponce, a Mexican engineer:

> He began, "I think you are a 'liberal woman.' Am I correct?" His expression meant to persuade me that it didn't matter what I replied. In the end he would win. He would systematically strip away all my pretexts, reservations and defenses, and end up in bed with me.
>
> In that country, the term "liberated woman" meant something other than what we had strived for back in the United States. In this case it simply meant a woman who would sleep nondiscriminately with any man who came along. I inhaled deeply from the strong cigarette he had given me and released the smoke in the direction of his face which diminished the sarcastic expression. (ML 73)

Caught once again between the dual anticipations of Mexican and U.S. values Teresa blows smoke at Ponce. Her response

represents one of the few instances where Castillo and her protagonist share a common point of view on a recurrent Chicana social
predicament.

Open Works

Much as Marjorie Shostak recommends that her readers reflect
critically on the limitations of ethnographic narrative and the tendency to universalize cultural difference, Castillo releases readers
from a prescribed reading and encourages them to become active
participants in her text. In an opening letter to the reader, she
proposes three possible readings of her novel, which "is not a book
to be read in the usual sequence. All letters are numbered to aid in
following any one of the author's proposed options: For the con-
formist; For the cynic; For the Quixotic." At the end of this letter
she alerts "the reader committed to nothing but short fiction [that]
all the letters read as separate entities. Good luck whichever journey you choose!" (ML n.p.). With this she releases readers from her
personal biases, her subjective interpretation.

Umberto Eco's concept of "open works" applies to both Castillo's and Shostak's productions. Open works are characterized by
movement and the invitation to assist the author in the making of
the text. These works are thus open to a continuous generation
of internal relations that the reader is encouraged to expose and
select in order to discover the text's totality. "Every work of art,
even though it is produced by following an explicit poetics of necessity, is effectively open to a virtually unlimited range of possible readings, each of which causes the work to acquire a new vi-
tality in terms of one particular taste, or perspective, or personal
performance.[13]

Castillo's and Shostak's open-work structure allows each to become an active participant in her cultural representation. Each in this way mediates not only between personal narrative and objective description, but also between the corresponding authorial roles as both creator and reader of her text. Through this mediation process both, in asides to the reader, raise questions of authority, authenticity, and interpretation that coincide with some of the major concerns in academe today. If we consider Shostak's *Nisa* an example of feminist ethnography, it is not farfetched to think of Castillo's text as metaethnography.

The primary difference between these two narrative projects is this: Shostak's seeks to portray culture, while Castillo's attempts to retaliate against social injustice and inequality. Both document the point of view of a single woman; neither "represent[s] the whole range of experience available to women in her culture." Castillo's narrative dramatizes the perils Chicanas confront when they defy authority and attempt to break away from the stagnant traditions and ideals that smother and suppress female desire, while Shostak's provides detailed descriptions that satisfy the reader's literary perceptions. Given that both texts explore the secrets and taboos of the female psyche in forms that are creative and profound, they can be read as sophisticated feminist challenges to patriarchal systems, alternative perspectives that expose and problematize the power of any outside or foreign "authority." *The Mixquiahuala Letters* and *Nisa* weave the imaginary and the real and show us how subjective experiences provide relevant strands of information essential to creating a space fundamental to any type of feminist practice. Both texts focus on women's culture, implying "that knowledge of the self as such can come only from acknowledging this special nature."[14]

5

Orality, Tradition, and Culture: Denise Chavez's *Novena Narrativas* and *The Last of the Menu Girls*

For if the word has the potency to revive and make us free, it also has the power to blind, imprison, and destroy.

RALPH ELLISON

They've always said, poor Indians they can't speak, so many speak for them. That's why I decided to learn Spanish.

RIGOBERTA MENCHÚ

Most Latinas, in looking to find some kind of literary tradition among our women, will usually speak of the "cuentos" our mothers and grandmothers told us. . . . The written word then becomes essential for communication when face-to-face contact is not possible.

ALMA GÓMEZ, CHERRÍE MORAGA,
AND MARIANA ROMO-CARMONA,
CUENTOS: STORIES BY LATINAS

A s the previous chapters illustrate, Chicana writers have used the force of the word to subvert a powerless cultural position that silence maintains. Speaking out, as this chapter's epigraphs suggest, entails an introspective process that begins with one's desire to represent oneself and gradually becomes a quest enhanced by the personal narratives of others. Even though most of us would agree that textual silences do not necessarily indicate a stagnant culture, we are nevertheless keenly aware of a correlation between print culture and one's station in life, aware that in today's world writing equates with power. Through the writings of Denise Chavez, in this chapter I explore the relationship between oral and print culture, tracking the narrative issues that emerge whenever a Chicana writer decides to shift from silence to print without dismissing the significance of oral culture.

In *Novena Narrativas,* a series of dramatic monologues, and *The Last of the Menu Girls,* a novel, Denise Chavez has produced two works that entice critics to reassess their conceptions of the oral tradition and ponder the relationship between gender, orality, domesticity, and Chicana narrative. Kathryn Rios notes that "in fiction and poetry, in testimonies and autobiographies, and in critical and theoretical works, silence seems to emerge as a discrete category in all genres of women's writing."[1] Chavez's writings not only reconfigure Chicana silence and invisibility into recognition and empowerment but highlight domestic orality and shatter dominant assumptions regarding women's textual silence(s) in general, which are all too often misinterpreted as reflecting a paucity of ideas. By employing both written and performance techniques, her works also allow readers to make important connections between oral traditions and the private, ritualistic practices of traditions and Chicano folk culture.[2]

The research of cultural critic Yolanda Broyles-González reflects similar concerns; her arguments call for a critical appraisal of the relationship between Chicano oral traditions and print culture. Exposing the limitations of conventional literary practices, which for the most part overlook or neglect oral traditions, Broyles-González urges Chicano literary critics to adopt an interdisciplinary approach that takes into account the work of folklorists and anthropologists who creatively engage the spoken word.

> "Orality" and "oral culture" are not merely references to "talk" or to spoken language. Rather, they encompass a form of human consciousness, a person's relationship to the surrounding organic world, a way of life. In oral cultures virtually all forms of human action happen in conjunction with verbal forms of exchange. Words have a physical presence, they are created by the human body, received aurally, and they are directly relevant to a lived set of circumstances.[3]

Broyles-González's commitment to the study of oral culture has enhanced her celebrated analysis of Teatro Campesino, which problematizes director/playwright Luis Valdez's representational practices by surveying the traditional, subordinate roles he has developed for women in the group.[4] "Women are first of all defined in a familial category: mother, grandmother, sister, or wife/girlfriend . . . divided into one of two sexual categories: whores or virgins."[5] Rather than taking on the role of "objective" authority, she develops a unique critique built on the oral testimonies of the women. One of Broyles-González's principal informants, Socorro Valdez, offers an interesting proposal for bringing multiple perspectives into the representation of women:

> My dream is to be able to do a theater piece on the phases of womanhood. It's something that has not been done yet.

All the times that I've seen women's programs or women in this or women in that, it somehow has never been quite satisfactory for me, you know. No one can take womanhood and put it into one thing. But that is precisely what I want to do. I want to put womanhood into every form that I can express: in singing, in crying, in laughing, everything. That role is not yet there. That role has not been written. . . . Women are obviously in a type of great void . . . they've put us in where we've accepted the condition of doing one role instead of many. If there were some way of taking that and putting it into words that are theatrical, I would like to do that. I don't believe a man is going to write that. I don't believe that for one single minute. And I sure can't wait for Luis to write that role.[6]

Socorro Valdez's aspirations not only coincide with those of Chicana social activists motivated by their desire to challenge patriarchal institutions, but also articulate a creative writer's solution that would use drama to encourage new levels of awareness.

Denise Chavez's writing claims new Chicano literary space by constructing a literary platform for women's experiences, by transforming Chicano *teatro* (and thereby helping bring Socorro Valdez's vision to life).[7]

The *Novena Narrativas*

In the *Novena Narrativas,* a series of dramatic monologues through which Chavez explores the "spirit of womanhood," a deity connects a variety of female characters and serves as the narratives'

center.[8] Chavez describes the work as "nine narrations to be per-
formed in monologue by one or more actresses. The characters vary
in age — from 7 to 78 — and are familiar to those of us who love
New Mexico, its traditions, cultures and daily life — full as it is with
significant detail."[9] The production features a family altar derived
from a complex set of cultural traditions that in the Southwest and
Latin America integrate storytelling, metaphysics, and spiritual of-
ferings. The new literary space delineated by the *Novena Narrativas* thus reflects, from an alternative (female) vantage point, a
fluid, culturally specific locale with the capacity to integrate symbolism, *indigenismo,* and Christianity.

Chavez's experimentation with aesthetic form breaks down
the artificial boundaries created by Western notions of religious
practice, revealing how the Roman Catholic church serves Latino
culture(s) as a base for active inquiry and reflection; in such cultures the statues of deities represent more than symbols eliciting
passive resignation. Consequently we begin to appreciate the way
a creative use of narrative form exposes new levels of symbolic
representation.

Chicana literary production has always occupied a marginal
position between white women's and Chicano and white men's
literature.[10] Partly because of this positioning, Chavez's work is
reminiscent of turn-of-the-century Anglo American women's literature that sought to explode dominant conceptions about women.
Speaking of the degrading choices that then confronted the literary
woman, Sandra Gilbert and Susan Gubar suggest that:

> she had to choose between admitting she was "only a
> woman" or protesting that she was "as good as a man"....
> The literature produced by women confronted with such

anxiety-inducing choices has been strongly marked not only by an obsessive interest in these limited options but also by obsessive imagery of confinement that reveals the ways in which female artists feel trapped and sickened both by suffocating alternatives and by the culture that created them.[11]

Even though Chavez's situation seems to resemble this one, upon closer consideration of the social climate in the United States, we must acknowledge that, in addition to their gender, women writers of color today also confront the degrading choices brought on by their racialized or ethnic status: More often than not they are positioned to choose between admitting that they are only "colored" women or protesting that they are as good as men.[12] Once we see that in this country racial/ethnic specificity determines one's social position, the relationship between contemporary Chicana literary production and its African American counterpart becomes apparent.

Similar to Broyles-Gonzáles's theoretical endeavors, Chavez's *Narrativas* calls on both the past (ritual) and the future (female solidarity) to deal with the gender/culture predicament; her perspective fluctuates between feminist intervention and the perpetuation of cultural stereotypes.[13] The mix includes the work's appreciation of Mexican oral traditions, folklore, and Chicana domesticity (which male writers often fail to consider). The *Narrativas* transcribes women's orality, documenting some of the daily circumstances that affect *la familia y la mujer* today and illustrating the relationship among women's contemporary activities, cultural rituals, and still-relevant traditions.[14] Synthesizing ancestral and modern perceptions, Chavez shows how Chicanas today fashion a cultural identity by combining traditional cultural attitudes with their postmodernist perceptions.

The *Novena Narrativas* curtain opens revealing a table, a chair, and a family altar fashioned on a tall chest. Covered in lace, the altar holds a statue of la Virgen de Guadalupe framed on the sides by two tall candles and in front by nine unlit votive candles.

> Isabel comes in breathlessly, with a bag of groceries that she sets down on the table. She leaves the food in the bag and organizes the area. The lights come down, and she throws the blanket on the floor, then lays down on it. She is tired and wants to meditate a while. It has been a busy day and she wants to relax. . . . After a long silence, in the darkness, she turns the lights up slightly and begins to exercise. She does various yoga positions. . . . With her back to the audience she begins talking. "Somebody asked me what I do for a living. I am an artist I said. I write. I am a writer." (NN 87)

With few spoken words the scene brings into play an oral culture wherein all action translates into verbal communication. Isabel's puffing activity, putting down her groceries and organizing the area, establishes the space as domestic before the character utters a single word. When we consider the underlying purpose of the practice of yoga — to reunite the body and the spirit — we can appreciate the complexity of Chavez's narrative project; like yoga it seeks to address our inability to discriminate between "the real and the unreal, that prevents us from realizing our true nature."[15]

In this opening interlude Chavez moves between the visual and spoken, alternating bits of information that oblige the audience to synthesize and interpret both modes of communication. We recognize Isabel as the writer/narrator of the play when her activity shifts from mumbling about the play and putting out the props to spontaneous rehearsal. Formally introducing herself to the audience, she comments on her status as woman artist. "My name is María Isabel González. . . . (sighing) When people tell me it's an easy time to be a woman, *me rio* [I laugh]! As far as I'm concerned, when you're a woman, no time is easy. And when you're an artist, it's worse" (NN 88).

The hint that women should begin to think of themselves in collective terms, as part of a female continuum rather than as isolated or singularly oppressed individuals, takes on weight as Isabel continues:

> When I feel alone, I remember behind me stand my grandmother, my mother, all the women who have come before me. Their spirits are always near, watching over me, guiding me, constantly teaching me. Today, when I went out for groceries, I heard one woman telling another, "La vida es una cancion." I could have sworn I heard my grama's voice. And then I thought: this woman is a thread that connects me to all women, everywhere. Wherever I go, I know the women. I know their deepest joys and pains. (NN 88)

To integrate generations of women, culture, and family, Chavez has her character state the obvious — that gender is the distinguishing characteristic that unifies all women. In addition, her use of the Spanish language invokes culture with the Mexican saying *La vida es una canción* (Life is a song) at the same time it invites the audience to consider its meaning. For the native speaker, the *dicho* (saying) connotes more than does its English translation, for it elicits memories of a national music (musical works, folk songs, dances created by individuals with close ties to a people) and of the cultural past, of folktales, of tradition — of *familia*.

Narrativas's nine female characters symbolize the nine days of devotion that constitute a novena in the Catholic religion: María Isabel González, the artist-narrator; Jesusita Rael, a storekeeper and spinster; Esperanza González, the wife of a Vietnam veteran; Minda Mirabal, a foster child; Magdalena Telles, an unwed mother of seven children; Tomasa Pacheco, a nursing-home resident; Juana Martinez, a factory employee; Pauline Mendoza, a teenager; and Corrine "La Cory" Delgado, a bag lady. Through them, Chavez lays out a variety of pressing issues, from the individual concerns of an elderly woman who reflects on her life without a husband, to larger societal problems that significantly distinguish the lives of her characters. These women from varying working-class experiences are held together by culture, religious ritual, and tradition.

Novena Narrativas enables Chavez to focus attention on the ideology of *Marianismo,* the cult that views women as semidivine, morally superior to and spiritually stronger than men. *Marianismo* has received short shrift in the literature, although much has been written about its counterpart in Mexican culture, *machismo*. The ideology is grounded in the Christian faith: To be a Marianist is to follow the model set by the Virgin Mary, the model of the self-sacrificing, and therefore spiritually superior, mother. Chicanos are socialized to become aggressive macho types, while women learn to maintain a complementary role of passivity and sacrifice. Because Chavez has redirected the public focus onto the private, personal relationship her female characters maintain with la Virgen de Guadalupe, her audience is introduced to the way in which Mexicans interpret Christianity and apply it to their lives. At the same time Chavez illuminates a daily, private, hidden, or overlooked segment of Chicano culture.

In *Novena Narrativas,* Denise Chavez orchestrates a cultural performance similar to that anthropologist Victor Turner describes in his studies on social drama, ritual, and performance—a traditional ethnographic project that solicits native informants to perform rituals and culture in a way that facilitates understanding for the anthropologist. Her sense of dialogue, understanding of setting and props, and ear for storytelling effectively assist an anthropological understanding of cultural meanings, indigenous rhetoric, and material culture; her characters dramatize their cultural perspectives on issues that pertain to gender, race, and class distinctions.[16]

The Last of the Menu Girls

Like *Novena Narrativas, The Last of the Menu Girls,* Chavez's novel composed of seven interrelated stories, employs multiple female voices to undermine essentialist notions about Chicanas and to depict what Socorro Valdez referred to as the "phases of womanhood" in Chicano culture. The title story introduces Chavez's protagonist and foreshadows the bildungsroman theme of the novel. As in *Narrativas* Chavez opens with a character who will function as the artist/narrator, Rocio Esquibel, a first-year university student interested in creative writing.

NAME: Rocio Esquibel

AGE: Seventeen

PREVIOUS EXPERIENCE WITH THE

    SICK AND DYING: My Great Aunt Eutilia

PRESENT EMPLOYMENT: Work-study aide at

    Altavista Memorial.[17]

Framed by this employment application, the story produces a series of direct questions that prompt a litany of female responses. (These personal narratives become a method for introducing character and plot in a way that reflects the influence of the theater and magical realism.) Describing her first interaction with her employer, Mr. Smith, Rocio shifts from dialogue to internal monologue.

Mr. Smith sat at his desk surrounded by requisition forms. He looked up to me with glassy eyes like filmy paperweights. MOTHER OF GOD, MR. SMITH WAS A WALLEYED HUNCHBACK! "Mr. Smith, I'm Rocio Esquibel, the workstudy student from the university and I was sent down here to talk to you about my job." "Down here, down here," he laughed, as if it were a private joke. "Oh, yes, you must be the new girl. Menus," he mumbled. "Now just have a seat and we'll see what we can do. Would you like some iced tea?" . . .

There was a bit of the gruesome Golom in him, a bit of the twisted spider in the dark. Was I to work for this gnome? I wanted to rescue souls, not play attendant to this crippled, dried up specimen, this cartilaginous insect with his misshapen head and eyes that peered out to me like the marbled eyes of statues one sees in museums. History preserves its freaks. God, was my job to do the same? No, never! (MG 18)

Rocio's responses are often fragmented and seem to defy time and space. Chavez's past/present reflections, her use of internal and external monologue set in contrast to dialogue, subverts a linear or sequential mode of storytelling. This narrative technique, grounded in Latin American literary tradition, also reflects how stories are one of the ways in which women give meaning to their lives.[18]

In the introduction to *Menu Girls* Rudolph Anaya welcomes Chavez into the ranks of writers, stating that her "feminine voice adds a new vision and dimension to the literature of this [Chicano] community." Certainly females, in their visibility and invisibility, pack the pages of this novel. The chapter "Shooting Stars," an extended reverie, unfolds by presenting to Rocio Esquibel a catalogue of female characters who first appear to her in the swirling surfaces of a wall. "The turning, plaster waves revealed my sisters, my mother, my cousins, my friends, their nude forms, half dressed, hanging out, lumpish, lovely, unaware of self, in rest rooms, in the dressing rooms, in the many stalls and the theaters of this life. I was the monitor of women's going forth. Behind the mirror, eyes half closed, I saw myself the cloud princess" (MG 64). As she watched, "one by one their faces broke out of the wall's textured surface and into my dreams to become living flesh and blood" — and to present a variety of female options for solving the riddle of female self-fashioning. "What did it mean to be a woman?" the protagonist has asked. "To be beautiful, complete? Was beauty a physical or a spiritual thing, was it strength of emotion, resolve, a willingness to love? What was it then, that made women lovely?" (MG 53). With vivid, fleeting female images Chavez describes "all those women": "All of them, they rise, then fall. Girls, girls, the bright beautiful girls, with white faces and white voices, they call out. They are shooting stars, shooting stars, spitting seeds. They are music, the echo of sound, the wind" (MG 65).

This passage is reminiscent of Charlotte Perkins Gilman's nineteenth-century narrative, *The Yellow Wallpaper,* with its depiction of the woman who creeps behind the wallpaper to escape the barricades that imprison her. Although both writers use walls to signify the limitations imposed on women, Chavez reflects the sentiment of the twentieth century by casting her women as shooting stars who through their rise and fall sow the seeds for change. She focuses our attention on movement, on the kinds of promise and change that a female sensibility can offer.

As in *Narrativas,* Chavez here also challenges mainstream assumptions by equating Mexican women with sound, orality. To say that girls "are music, the echo of sound, the wind," seems to suggest that, as Ana Castillo wrote, "women are not roses," that things are not always what they appear to be.

Menu Girls also features the mundane domestic realities that for whatever reason seem to be overlooked or considered inappropriate for public discussion. In "The Closet" Chavez invites readers to explore the forgotten or uncelebrated household spaces that are synonymous with the female position in U.S. society.

Standing in the closet I can smell mother, all of her, forty-eight years old in her flowered bathrobes, and suits of gradually increasing girth. It is the soft, pungent woman smell of a fading mother of three girls, one of them the daughter of the unfortunate Juan Luz. In the darkness there is the smell of my mother's loneliness. Next to me the portrait of my mother and Juan Luz is hidden behind piles of clothes which are crowded into the house's largest

closet. All those memories are now suffocated in cloth.
(MG 80)

A woman, like a closet, is private, functional, and often overlooked, yet like a closet she can facilitate new levels of organization.

Rocio's detailed recollections also remind readers of the political implications of visibility.

> The things that we imagine support us never do. The
> world takes us quickly, handles us harshly, splinters us,
> casts us down and sends us forward to more pain. And yet,
> when I play back the tape, Mercy, I always play back love,
> much love.
>
> I hear voices that say: "We are the formless who take
> form, briefly, in rooms, and then wander on. We are the
> grandmothers, aunts, sisters. We are the women who love
> you."
>
> "Oh my God, Mercy, do you understand these things?"
> No amount of tears will ever wash the pain or translate the
> joy. Over and over, it's the same, then as now. Birth and
> Death. There's me, in the Grey Room, or in the closet with
> the shoes.
>
> "Mercy, remember the closets, remember them?" (MG
> 85)

Rocio justifies the lack of female visibility in the culture with the
romantic notion that women are the loving mortals who respond
to pain with love. Her admonition to always "remember the clos-
ets" is a subtle reminder of the ideology of *Marianismo* and the
legacy of women's superiority through submission and invisibility.

With a perspective that seems both to pose and answer feminist questions concerning visibility and control, Chavez develops a narrative that privileges reflection, internal monologue, and dialogue. Yet even though she seems to idealize love and private spaces with the implication that women should step into the closet of anonymity, that containment and invisibility are analogous to spiritual freedom and moral superiority, we would be wrong to deny the liberating elements of her text. In a complex project that holds the potential for representing alternative interpretations of tradition and order, Chavez attempts a new literary form and at the same time contributes to a Latina literary tradition that consolidates cultural traditions and feminist concerns.

New Visions: Gender and Beyond

Beyond her creative treatment of the gender vs. culture dilemma that confronts many Chicana writers today, beyond her privileging of domestic space(s) as a metaphor for women's limitation and subordination, Denise Chavez makes all categories of the oppressed the focus of her art and in doing so liberates her readers from much more than their misconceptions about domesticity. *Menu Girls* offers a kaleidoscope of images and issues that pertain equally to Chicanas, Chicanos, and Mexicanos in the United States.

The opening chapter, "The Last of the Menu Girls," introduces themes that recur throughout the novel, among them racism, religion, self-contempt, and homophobia. Altavista Hospital, a microcosm of working-class Chicano reality that could be any county hospital in the United States that serves a Chicano/Latino population, is the site of Rocio Esquibel's first work-study experience. The hospital and her observation there set the tone for a coming-of-age novel that punctuates "difference" with a variety of cultural reflections and interpretations.

Through references and extended discussions of boundaries and space, Chavez subtly raises issues of the border culture, restrictions, and migrant farm labor. In "Willow Game," she weaves the concerns of a child with the reflections of a cultural critic.

> I was a child before there was a South. That was before the magic of the East, the beckoning North, or the West's betrayal. For me there was simply Up the street toward the spies' house, next to Old Man W's or there was Down, past the Marking-Off Tree in the vacant lot that was the shortcut between worlds. Down was the passageway to family, the definition of small self as one of the whole, part of a past. Up was in the direction of town, flowers. (MG 41)

The final chapter, "Compadre," reflects a shift in time and voice as it develops a more sustained analysis of border issues.

> East and west were the boundaries of the town, the farms of chile and cotton; east and west were intimations of space and proof of relatives who still clung to the land, and who were revered by the landlocked majority as part of a dying past. North was a point beyond knowing; it led to large cities, other cultures, a difference in climate. (MG 152)

This chapter is significant for a number of reasons. It breaks with literary tradition by continuing to integrate new characters, which both extends Chavez's narrative concerns and expresses universal questions that relate to silence and domesticity. Her depiction of Eleiterio, a quiet young friend of the family, asks readers to reconsider the domestic sphere and the power relations that overdetermine one's public persona.

> As a matter of fact, when given a moment of calm recollection, I never could remember the timbre or tone of his voice. When he spoke, all sound stopped and out of vacuum I imagined sound and some sense of form. I heard his voice, but the hearing was nothing to be registered or even recalled, except with a disconcerting memory of absolute stillness. I do not remember Eleiterio's voice at all. No doubt it was quiet, with a certain halting inflection of someone not used to speaking. It was the voice of someone usually mute, stilled by a life in a house full of women, women and one other man. (MG 165)

Adding men to her narrative allows Chavez to escape or perhaps resist the limitations of binary opposition. "Compadre" plays with a number of other role reversals as it explores cultural values that range from the concept of *compadrazco,* a form of close, spiritual connection that resembles and sometimes goes beyond family bonding, to *verguenza,* a cultural signifier for shame.

Literary/Cultural Challenges

Because Chavez's narrative strategies challenge literary order, they enable others to explore the terrain of everyday practices. *The Last of the Menu Girls* and *Novena Narrativas* provide a potpourri of cultural challenges and women's perspectives that reflect values and culture specific to New Mexico. Transforming the religious ritual of the novena into a creative female form of expression — the *novena narrativa* — delicately and politely raises feminist questions. But even though the Roman Catholic church's patriarchal ideology, ritualistic practices, and emphasis on the cult of *Marianismo* are fruitful terrain for feminist inquiry, the *Novena Narrativas* declines to plow this ground. With a nostalgia typical of the cultural nationalist rhetoric of the 1960s, Chavez instead tries, as she has said, to "link New Mexico to the universal spirit of womanhood." What might have been a feminist intervention is reduced to a celebratory testament to women's inequality. In the final analysis, Chavez's new form gives her the flexibility to hold the focus on "the spirit of womanhood" while reinforcing traditional (that is, masculine) cultural values and mores.

Yet we must admit that radical feminism is not necessarily relevant to all Chicanas, that women can challenge the confines of patriarchy on many levels. Chavez's writing is sophisticated and complex in its accurate portrayal of the ideological perspectives that prevail in New Mexico. She raises important questions that set parameters for further inquiry and contestation. On one hand, she defies traditional literary form by calling attention to a feminine, cultural space that has been overlooked or forgotten. On the other, by placing la Virgen de Guadalupe as the central deity in her female-centered narratives, she conforms to the Mexican ideological structures that shape a cultural system with only two models for women: the pure, self-sacrificing wife, mother, girlfriend, or *la mala mujer* (the evil woman). Yet on another level this narrative approach sets the stage for a sustained cultural analysis that holds the potential for change. What we need to keep in mind when we read Chavez is that she writes to open rather than close discussions on culture and gender, that she sees both categories as active rather than stagnant. Although she fails to propose concrete solutions, she seems to summon creative interpretation and movement, as indicated by her experimentation with literary form.

What Chavez finally reveals through the production of her text is the tension between female and feminist representation.[19] *Narrativas* seems to represent an earnest entreaty for the recognition of a particular female role in Mexican culture, a Chicana/Mexicana presence that is varied and polyphonic. Furthermore, with her synthesis of oral and print modes in *Narrativas* Chavez has contributed to a new "teatroesque" literature. As a writer and cultural critic her literary agenda seems to confirm Victor Turner's conclusion that "if daily living is a kind of theater, social drama is a kind of metatheatre, that is a dramaturgical language about the language of ordinary role-playing and status-maintenance which constitutes communication in the quotidian social process."[20]

Chavez's social position as a Chicana writer influences her determination to write about culture and gender in a way that represents difference and challenges mainstream assumptions. Her original narrative approach thus contributes to a resistance literature that in Barbara Harlow's terms "expands the formal criteria of closure and continuity which characterize the ideology of traditional plots and subjects the images of tradition to analytical inquiry."[21]

6

New Visions: Culture, Sexuality, and Autobiography

> What began as a reaction to the racism of white femi-
> nists soon became a positive affirmation of the commit-
> ment of women of color to our *own* feminism. Mere
> words on a page began to transform themselves into a
> living entity in our guts.[1]

With the 1981 publication of *This Bridge Called My Back: Writings by Radical Women of Color*, Cherríe Moraga and Gloria Anzaldúa helped launch an oppositional movement centered on the perspectives of women of color. Inspired by feelings of alienation and exclusion, the anthology articulated an alternative to Anglo-American feminism, which, due to its exclusive appropriation of the category "woman," disregarded race, ethnicity, and class as modes of female subjectivity.

Reflecting on the anthology's theoretical impact, Norma Alarcón suggests that "*Bridge* along with eighties writings by many women of color in the United States has problematized many a version of Anglo-American feminism and has helped open the way for alternate feminist discourses and theories."[2] Teresa de Lauretis links *Bridge* with *All the Women Are White, All the Blacks Are Men, but Some of Us Are Brave*, edited by Gloria Hull, Patricia Bell

Scott, and Barbara Smith, as important texts "that first made available to all feminists the feelings, the analyses, the political positions of feminists of color, and their critiques of white or mainstream feminism."[3] Most critics, like Alarcón and de Lauretis, correctly laud the book as a distinct cultural product that contributed to new levels of understanding. In this chapter, however, I would like to evaluate it less as a product than as a symbol of a sociocultural process, keeping in mind Moraga's comments from the 1981 edition:

> Change does not occur in a vacuum. In this preface I have tried to recreate for you my own journey of struggle, growing consciousness, and subsequent politicization and vision as a woman of color. I want to reflect in actual terms how this anthology and the women in it and around it have personally transformed my life, sometimes rather painfully but always with richness and meaning.[4]

As an anthology of the personal and collective struggles of a variety of women of color, *Bridge* is a cooperative project inspired by an idea nurtured and brought to fruition under the guidance of editors Cherríe Moraga and Gloria Anzaldúa. The product and its writers (re)politicize and challenge mainstream feminist agendas. Its production heightened awareness about the limitations of essentialist rhetoric and led to a consideration of a number of important ideological concerns regarding racism, classism, colonialism, imperialism, and heterosexism.

As Moraga suggests in *Bridge,* "each woman considers herself a feminist, but draws her feminism from the culture in which she grew."[5] In "The Theoretical Subject(s) of *This Bridge Called My Back* and Anglo-American Feminism," Norma Alarcón (one of the writers included in *Bridge*) analyzes the text's reception among women of color and Anglo feminists. While women of color respond favorably because the text speaks to them, Anglo feminist readers "tend to appropriate it, cite it as an instance of difference between women, and proceed to negate that difference by subsuming women of color into the unitary category of woman/women."[6] Alarcón's discussion lays the groundwork for subsequent studies of the mainstream's tendency to emphasize product over process. This theoretical practice poses particular epistemological problems for Anglo-feminists, who through their politically unconscious application of the dicta of Western civilization, with its claims of emotion-free objectivity, negate the politics, emotions, and process by which the discourse on women of color is based. Unfortunately, this tendency steers mainstream theorists away from developing a comprehensive analysis of *Bridge* that takes into account both production and the emergent (oppositional) feminist consciousness reflected in the text's themes.

I suggest here a dual focus on product and production that will allow us to look at how socially constructed "difference" compels women of color to organize and challenge dominant practices. More specifically, consider the way Cherríe Moraga and Gloria Anzaldúa in their autobiographies *Loving in the War Years* and *Borderlands/La Frontera* transform many of *Bridge*'s themes and narrative strategies into sustained methods for Chicana feminist self-fashioning. This analysis will permit us both to track the social formation of two prominent Chicana feminist theorists and to trace the shifts in political awareness that differentiate feminists of color from the mainstream.

Toni Cade Bambara concludes the foreword that appears in both editions of *Bridge* with a statement that provides a springboard for an analysis of the two autobiographies:

Quite frankly, *This Bridge* needs no Foreword. It is the Afterward that'll count . . . the contracts we creative combatants will make to mutually care and cure each other into wholesomeness . . . the blue-prints we will draw up of the new order we will make manifest . . . the personal unction we will discover in the mirror, in the dreams, or on the path across *This Bridge*. The work: To make revolution irresistible.[7]

In coordinating the voices and experiences of many women writers of color, Moraga and Anzaldúa were among the first to produce a text that contemplated critical issues concerning the relationship between linguistics, identity politics, sexuality, cultural heterogeneity, and hybridity — categories of *difference* that surpass simplistic binary paradigms. As coeditors they orchestrated content and form to depict a model of female subjectivity based on a variety of social experiences. José Saldívar tells us that *Loving in the War Years* and *Borderlands/La Frontera* represent the "first sustained models of radical Chicana feminist theories."[8] This implies that, in Bambara's terms, Moraga and Anzaldúa, through the production of their personal narratives, have extended the *Bridge* agenda and provided "the blue-prints" that help make "revolution irresistible."

Loving in the War Years: Lo Que Nunca Paso por Sus Labios

In the introduction to *Loving in the War Years,* Cherríe Moraga uses the image of her grandmother to establish the central focus of her text. The imminent death of the grandmother stirs an aware-

ness of the impending loss of everything she symbolizes, most specifically language, tradition, and culture.[9] "And what goes with
her?" Moraga asks. "My claim to an internal dialogue where *el
gringo* does not penetrate? *Su memoria a de noventa y seis años*
[her memory of ninety-six years] going back to a time where
'*nuestra cultura*' [our culture] was not the subject of debate. *I write
this book because we are losing ourselves to the gabacho* [gringo]"
(emphasis in the original).[10] Apart from defining her purpose, in
the opening pages Moraga also sheds light on the relationship for
her between writing and self-discovery. A seven-year developmen-
tal process that takes her from Los Angeles, where she was "living
out my lesbianism as a lie on my job and a secret to my family," to
Berkeley, San Francisco, Boston, Mexico, and finally Brooklyn,
where she came "out-to-the-world" in print. The opening thus lays
the foundation for the dual principles of desire and narrative form
woven throughout the book, encompassing the ideological struggle, resistance, and warfare that arise from cultural, racial/ethnic,
and sexual subordination.

Even though Moraga in *Loving* speaks only for herself, explaining "that is all this really is/can be — my story," the narrative
represents the concerns of a larger political category and resonates
with many of the central issues evident in *Bridge*. Moraga, who is
aware of this interpretation but uncomfortable about speaking on
behalf of a community, cites a friend's comment that reconsiders
the dilemma for her: "There's really no such thing as community
among *politicos*. Community is simply the way people live a life
together. And they're doing it all over the world. The only way to
write for *la comunidad* is to write so completely from your heart
what is your own personal truth. This is what touches people"
(L vi). To present her story Moraga masterfully blurs literary
genres, synthesizing essays, poems, short stories, and *testimonio* (in

a form similar to that of *Bridge*) to convey a variety of voices, perspectives, and limitations that inform her complex subject position.

In "La Guera" (The Fair One), an essay that originally appeared in *Bridge,* Moraga introduces herself as the well-educated daughter of a functionally illiterate Chicana. "My mother was born in Santa Paula, Southern California, at a time when much of the central valley there was still farm land. Nearly thirty-five years later, in 1948, she was the only daughter of six to marry an anglo, my father" (L 50). The essay describes Moraga's socialization through formal and informal education, which contributed to her awareness about white-skin privilege and the kind of deception that would guarantee success as long as she pretended to be white, upwardly mobile, and heterosexual. "La Guera" raises one of the text's central concerns, depicting the factors that contributed to Moraga's initial acceptance of dominant ideology and her subsequent political awakening.

> When I finally lifted the lid to my lesbianism, a profound connection with my mother reawakened in me. It wasn't until I acknowledged and confronted my own lesbianism in the flesh, that my heartfelt identification with and empathy for my mother's oppression — due to being poor, uneducated, and Chicana — was realized. My lesbianism is the avenue through which I have learned the most about silence and oppression, and it continues to be the most tactile reminder to me that we are not free human beings. (L 52)

She continues by challenging her readers to explore and perhaps even name the enemy they may hold within: "In this country, lesbianism is a poverty — as is being brown, as is being a woman, as is being just plain poor. The danger lies in ranking the oppressions. The danger lies in failing to acknowledge the specificity of the oppression. The danger lies in attempting to deal with oppression purely from a theoretical base" (L 52).

Moraga goes on to raise sophisticated theoretical concerns about the limitations of dispassionate rhetoric and to introduce her own resolution—theoretical poetics. She uses poetry to arouse the emotions and feelings more often than not suppressed when we privilege or overrely on "theory," and she disputes mainstream feminist assumptions by suggesting that "we have let rhetoric do the job of poetry. Even the word 'oppressor' has lost its power. We need a new language, better words that can more closely describe women's fear of and resistance to one another; words that will not always come out sounding like dogma" (L 54).

A continual juxtaposing of poetry and prose coerces readers to do the obscene, to engage in synchronous feeling and thinking, to blend the emotional and analytical. In an essay Moraga asserts that "even the word 'oppression' has lost its power"; in a subsequent poem, she warns that "to gain the word to describe the loss, I risk losing everything." Here is the stanza from "It's the Poverty" in which she describes the tensions and some of the contradictions that result from language.

> Words are a war to me.
> They threaten my family.
> To gain the word to describe the loss,
> I risk losing everything,
> I may create a monster,
> the word's length and body
> swelling up colorful and thrilling
> looming over my mother, characterized.

> Her voice in the distance
> *unintelligible illiterate.*
> These are the monster's words. (L 63)

The connections Moraga makes between desire, politics, and narrative are built on a series of love poems that highlight sexuality and *difference.* The content of the poetry transforms the genre into a form of resistance that, with its candid expression, represents a passion set in dialectical opposition to mainstream, heterosexist perceptions. Moraga takes readers on an emotional tour that begins with the erotic passion of a love that challenges dominant assumptions because it opposes "societal norms" and thus guarantees struggle and warfare, as the titles of some of her poems seem to suggest — "Loving in the War Years," "Loving on the Run," "Fear, A Love Poem."

Once Moraga has established an emotional foundation, she switches genres to refine her analysis. With the short story "Pesadilla" (Nightmare) she executes a textual shift that expands her cultural critique to explore the intersections between race, gender, and sexual oppression. The story's opening, set in italics, sets up one of the narrative's central themes.

> There came the day when Cecilia began to think about color. Not the color of trees or painted billboards or the magnificent spreads of color laid down upon the hundreds of Victorians that lined the streets of her hometown city. She began to think about skin color. And the thought took hold of her and would not give; would not let loose. So that every person — man, woman, and child — had its particular grade of shade. And that meant all the difference in the world . . . nothing seemed fair to her anymore; the war,

the rent, the prices, the weather. And it spoiled her time.
(L 36)

The story of two lesbian lovers of color, "Pesadilla" describes
Cecilia's initiation into an American reality founded on color consciousness and social injustice. Cecilia and Deborah move into a
small apartment in Brooklyn, believing that their love will rescue
the dwelling from its previous incarnation of rage, poverty, and
filth. As the story evolves, terror overwhelms the lovers' romantic
naiveté when they return to their freshly cleaned and painted apartment to discover that someone has broken in and shattered their
dreams.

> What kind of beast they cried would do this? His parts
> drawn all over their freshly painted walls for them to see
> and such and that's what he told them there on the wall.
>
> SUCK MY DICK   YOU HOLE
>
> He had wanted money and finding no such thing, but a
> picture of a woman who could have been a sister or a lover
> or a momma and no sign of man around, he wrote:
>
> I'M BLACK YOU MOTHERFUCKER BITCH
>
> YOU BUTCH (L 38)

"Pesadilla" dramatizes Moraga's profound critique of white supremacy and the dominant ideology that systematically destroys
potential and promise, eliciting both the inner-city black man's
angry reaction and Cecilia's and Deborah's cognition of their powerless status. Cecilia has a nightmare that contributes to her insecurity and awareness of her lack of power as a person of color under
white patriarchy. "The feeling that she could not shake, was of
some other presence living amongst them. Some white man some-

where—their names always mono-syllabled: Tom, Dick, Jack" (L 40).

Moraga documents Cecilia's deteriorating optimism and finally her conclusion that women are pawns, "daughters" of white, male supremacy. The story portrays Cecilia's rude awakening into the "real" world of inequality and hatred. Moraga casts this coming of age as an American nightmare that converts dreams of freedom, love, and potential into disillusionment and fear. We come to understand that Cecilia's conclusion that nothing seems fair develops hand in hand with her awareness that her welfare is based on her gender and skin color. Sadly, her perception represents a sign of her emotional maturation as a person of color living in the United States.

> Cecilia didn't understand why her feelings were changing, only that they had to change. Change or die, she thought. And suddenly she grew stiff and fixed in her chair, hands pressed between her knees, riveted against the tide of rage and regret she knew her mother's memories would call forth. Old wounds still oozing with the blood of sinners in wartime. (L 41)

Moraga's *cuento* functions as an allegory about color and race consciousness, depicting the paradox that links consciousness raising with immobilization, fear, and limitation; it reiterates Moraga's central focus on the relationship between identity and race, class, culture, and gender oppression.

The final section of the book, "Lo Que Nunca Paso Por Sus Labios" (That Which Has Never Passed through Your Lips), includes a long essay, "A Long Line of Vendidas" (Traitors), dedicated to Gloria Anzaldúa. In an interview with Norma Alarcón,

Moraga describes the audience she had in mind for it. "It was the most recently written chapter. I knew who I was writing to. I felt like it was very much to Chicanos, and to Latinos, and then to Third World people — that's how I broke it down. But I was aware that White people were going to read it initially, which is what happened to *Bridge*."[11]

In "A Long Line of Vendidas," the only footnoted chapter in the book, Moraga develops an intricate analysis of Chicana/o culture, taking on with a grand-finale quality a series of provocative subjects presented earlier in the text, including history, myth, cultural nationalism, radical feminism, and Chicana feminist practices. The nonchronological sequence of the earlier writing in *Loving* is maintained here, sustaining Moraga's "emotional/political chronology" (L i) through a composite of childhood recollections, critical analysis, metahistory, and journal entries.

Out of Moraga's complex social predicament brought about by her bicultural, light-skin status, she speaks in "Vendidas" of internal oppression and a cultural schizophrenia that seems to simultaneously encourage and denigrate passing for white. Blending the personal and the political, she illuminates some of the cultural pressures and attitudes that install a fear of difference.

> To write as a Chicana feminist lesbian, I am afraid of being mistaken, of being made an outsider again — having to fight the kids at school to get them to believe Teresita and I were cousins. "You don't look like cousins!" I feel at times I am trying to bulldoze my way back into a people who forced me to leave them in the first place, who taught me to take my whiteness and run with it. Run with it. Who want nothing to do with me, the likes of me, the white me — in them. (L 95)

The overarching metaphor of this entire last chapter is the archetypal myth of cultural betrayal. In the essay "A Long Line of Vendidas" Moraga weaves a sophisticated history of the systematic subordination and control of women that began (as masculinist historiography tells) at the Conquest with a native woman named Malintzin Tenepal (La Malinche). She argues eloquently that "it is this myth of the inherent unreliability of women, our natural propensity for treachery, which has been carved into the very bone of Mexican/Chicano collective psychology. Traitor begets traitor" (L 101).[12]

Beyond the culturally specific discussions of women's oppression, "Vendidas" offers an equally extensive analysis of mainstream and Chicana feminist discourse, featuring one of the first sustained comparisons of the 1960s Chicano, black cultural nationalist, and women's movements. Moraga repeatedly attests to the limitations of Anglo-feminist practices. "White women's feminism did little to answer my questions. As a Chicana feminist my concerns were different." The essay proclaims her commitment to three distinct communities — lesbian, Chicano and white — while offering readers an "insider's critique" of radical-feminist, cultural-nationalist, and dominant patriarchal ideology. "Vendidas" thus gives readers new translations that actively interrogate oppositional rhetoric and encourage a consideration of dominant notions of sexuality, culture, and history.

Ultimately, Moraga's autobiography functions as a symbolic act of resistance: It represents her coming out to the world and her open love for *la mujer*, her language, her culture. The identity quest that began with a realization about sexuality and led to inevitable banishment from mother, home, and culture brings her full circle to the site of her initial estrangement — home. Ironically, the narrative reveals that it was the love of her mother that instilled the forbidden passion she feels for women — the love of *la mujer* and *la cultura,* the love she was forced to suppress in order to survive. Her discursive "coming out" symbolizes a rebirth that transgresses patriarchal limitations and claims her right to love, language, and culture. "In returning to the love of my race, I must return to the fact that not only has the mother been taken from me, but her tongue, her mother tongue. I want the language, feel my tongue rise to the occasion of feeling at home, in common. I know this language in my bones" (L 141).

On a personal level the self-explorations depicted in Moraga's autobiography raise a number of critical issues that facilitate her self-fashioning as a biracial, Chicana, lesbian feminist from California. She has traded her feelings of powerlessness and cultural ambivalence for a newfound wisdom. "I am a lesbian. And I am a Chicana. . . . These are two inseparable facts of my life. I can't talk or write about one without the other" (L 142). But when we reflect on the narrative form and content of *Loving in the War Years,* it becomes evident that Moraga has also helped prepare both the Anglo American feminist and Chicana/o audience for Gloria Anzaldúa's meditations in her autobiography, *Borderlands/La Frontera.* While Moraga initiates a discussion about women's oppression with an implication of cultural and regional specificity, Anzaldúa develops a sustained analysis of the relationship between indigenous, Mexican, Chicano, and Anglo American cultures.

Borderlands/La Frontera: The New Mestiza

Cherríe Moraga's *Loving in the War Years* reveals intense passion and a quest for culture, language, and self-understanding, qualities that must have contributed to Moraga's close, productive association with Gloria Anzaldúa, coauthor of *This Bridge Called My Back,* who for her part seems to have helped fill at least a portion of the cultural void Moraga first associated (in her text) with the death of her grandmother.

If we reflect on the individual contributions each author makes to *Bridge,* it becomes apparent that, although both are Chicana lesbians, they can be more profoundly characterized by their differences than their similarities. Moraga introduces in the first four sections categories that in general terms could have provided a thematic outline for her subsequent autobiography: "The Roots of Our Radicalism," "Theory in the Flesh," "Racism in the Women's Movement," and "On Culture, Class, and Homophobia." Anzaldúa introduces the final two sections — "The Third World Woman Writer" and "The Vision of the Third World Feminist" — which help establish a foundation for the racial, ritualistic, and cultural issues deeply embedded in *La Frontera.*

The textual personas each woman establishes indirectly recreate the European/indigenous opposition that resulted from the European invasion and conquest of Meso-America. "La Guera" (The Fair One) discloses a life of white-skin privilege and the struggles that came as a result of her *passing,* Anzaldúa's "La Prieta" (The Dark One) conveys disapproval and the disadvantages guaranteed by her dark complexion.

> When I was born, Mamagrande Locha inspected my buttocks looking for the dark blotch, the sign of *indio,* or worse, of mulatto blood. . . . Too bad *mihijita* was *morena, muy prieta,* so dark and different from her own fair-skinned children. But she loved *mihijita* anyway. What I

lacked in whiteness, I had in smartness. But it was too bad I was dark like an Indian.[13]

Moraga's white skin provides an avenue for escape and denial; Anzaldúa's dark skin obliges her either to indulge in a destructive self-contempt or to acknowledge and embrace the Indian she holds within. She chooses the embrace: "My Chicana identity is grounded in the Indian woman's history of resistance."[14]

The differences revealed by the Moraga and Anzaldúa auto-biographies illustrate the array of regional, social, and cultural influences that can contribute to Chicana multiple subjectivity. Anzaldúa's text incorporates Moraga's concerns within the context of cultural difference(s); it reifies hybridity and creolization by transforming the Mexican concept of *mestizaje* into a textual metaphor — the borderlands.

Linking personal experience, self-identity, sexuality, historiography, and regionality in *La Frontera,* Anzaldúa expands and dramatizes the erotic/textual standards Moraga negotiates by integrating poetry and prose. As does Moraga's autobiography, Anzaldúa's documents the author's personal reflections on identity politics, illustrating how the process of writing has provided stability in her life.

When I don't write the images down for several days or weeks or months, I get physically ill. Because writing invokes images from my unconscious, and because some of the images are residues of trauma which I then have to reconstruct, I sometimes get sick when I do write. I can't stomach it, become nauseous, or burn with fever, worsen. But, in reconstructing the traumas behind the images, I

make "sense" of them, and once they have "meaning" they
are changed, transformed. It is then that writing heals me,
brings me great joy. (LF 70)

Moraga's and Anzaldúa's personal narratives augment their co-
edited anthology, creating a dialogue (like that among the narrative
voices in *Bridge*) that speaks of fluidity rather than stagnation.
Their individual cultural critiques, like those of the Third World
women writers they consolidated in *Bridge,* help facilitate innovative theoretical practices. But rather than focus on the obvious
textual similarities *Loving in the War Years* and *La Frontera* register, I propose to consider some significant ideological differences.

One variation results from the way these authors arrange
their self-representations. Anzaldúa's "women-centered" narrative
agenda contrasts dramatically with the feminist theoretical concerns highlighted in Moraga's text. Anzaldúa initiates an analysis
of self with a tribute to the earth — *la tierra*. In a poetic counterdiscourse, she suggests that the earth resembles women in that it
offers a source from which to develop transformative stories. Anzaldúa uses *la tierra* as a foundation for an experimental autobiography that marks her attempt to rewrite history and myth.
Although both writers articulate feminist oppositional perspectives, Anzaldúa seems to register more of an early women's studies/
cultural nationalist consciousness-raising sentiment whose fore-
most aim is bolstering self-esteem.[15] Her self-fashioning quest,
complicated by a commitment to women and to ancient indigenous culture, has inspired her to reconsider masculinist interpretations of *indigenismo* (indigenous discourse) and coerced her to
develop alternative myths that take into account the experiences
and influences of women.

Anzaldúa's project resembles that of Alurista, Chicano poet laureate of the 1960s, whom many critics have credited with generating the cultural nationalist call for a return to the indigenous homeland. Anzaldúa's opening chapter, "The Homeland, Aztlan/ *El Otro Mexico,*" rearticulates Alurista's call in the rhetoric of the 1980s; because of its focus on women, her alternative rendition of history and myth creatively shifts the reader's attention from the masculinist representations that generally dominate nationalism. In different terms, Anzaldúa's autobiography reinterprets and reappropriates that which has been defined and appropriated by men. Although much has been written about Aztlan and Aztec mythology, Gloria Anzaldúa's *La Frontera* is one of the few Chicana feminist interventions to redefine the "indigenous spiritual homeland" in women's terms.

Grounding her personal narrative in the earth, from which she and her people evolved, enables Anzaldúa to trace backwards its cultural history. She evokes the Texas/Mexican border, with its legacy as a site of political struggle, as her central metaphor. This narrative strategy brilliantly sets the stage for Anzaldúa's discussion in her preface of artificial boundaries and multiple levels of cultural resistance.

> The actual physical borderland that I'm dealing with in this book is the Texas-U.S. Southwest/Mexican border. The psychological borderlands, the sexual borderlands and the spiritual borderlands are not particular to the Southwest. In fact, the Borderlands are physically present wherever two or more cultures edge each other, where people of different races occupy the same territory, where under, lower, middle and upper classes touch, where the

space between two individuals shrinks with intimacy. (LF, preface)

Anzaldúa's provocative border metaphor has generated an enormous amount of critical attention and stimulated interest in Latino diasporic studies beyond the Southwest. Anthropologist Renato Rosaldo argues that Anzaldúa has developed and transformed "the crossroads in a manner that celebrates the potential of borders in opening new forms of understanding."[16] Sonia Saldívar Hull, in "Feminism on the Border," reflects on the interconnections between sexuality, gender oppression, and Chicano patriarchal traditions, offering a marvelous illustration of the new forms of understanding Anzaldúa's border metaphor facilitates. "Anzaldúa's project problematizes further still the traditions of Chicanismo, when as a lesbian Chicana, she forces the homophobes of the Chicano community to see their prejudice. If the heterosexual Chicana is ostracized from her culture for transgressing its rules of behavior, for the Chicana lesbian the ultimate rebellion she can make against her native culture is through her sexual behavior."[17] José Saldívar equates Anzaldúa's national-border allegory with the author's experimentation with literary genre, suggesting that "suddenly at the beginning of her life history, we no longer are in a prototypical conversion/autobiographical confession mode, but in ritual."[18]

Unlike Moraga's text, which integrates a variety of literary forms, *Borderlands/La Frontera*'s two sections roughly break down into prose and poetry. But this distinction lacks edges, because Anzaldúa's prose is highly poetic in structure as well as content, and like poetry it always begins with feeling. With the opening section, "*Atravesando Fronteras*/Crossing Borders," however, comes a striking linguistic variation that the author has prepared us for in the preface: "The switching of 'codes' in this book from English to Castillian Spanish to the North Mexican dialect to Tex-Mex to a sprinkling of Nahuatl to a mixture of all of these, reflects my language, a new language—the language of the Borderlands" (LF, preface). Anzaldúa's confident prose conveys her comfort and competence with history, mythology, and the language(s) of the border—Spanish, English, and Nahuatl. The writing epitomizes *mestizaje*; in a mosaic that maneuvers the reader, its narrative practices limit and control understanding for monolingual speakers of English. Anzaldúa seems at home in her role as cultural hostess: "This book is our invitation to you—from the new *mestizas*."

Although Moraga goes unacknowledged in Anzaldúa's text, her influence is immediately apparent. In fact, it can be quite productive to read *Borderlands/La Frontera* as a response to *Loving in the War Years,* for Anzaldúa contemplates and expands upon Moraga's cultural analysis. The first subtle reference to Moraga's narrative appears with the title of Chapter two, "Movimientos *de* Rebeldia y Las Culturas que Traicionan" (Resistance Movements and Cultures of Betrayal). Beginning on a note that resonates with Moraga's "A Long Line of Vendidas," Anzaldúa discusses Mexicano/Chicano homophobic cultural values and her inevitable flight from home.

> To this day I'm not sure where I found the strength to leave the source, the mother, disengage from my family, *mi tierra, mi gente,* and all that picture stood for. I had to leave home so I could find myself, find my own intrinsic nature buried under the personality that had been imposed on me. (LF 16)

Her exodus corresponds with the self-imposed cultural exile Moraga describes. But distancing her experience from that of Moraga, Anzaldúa meticulously recounts a cultural awareness she equates with her socialization as a Tejana (Texan).

> I feel perfectly free to rebel and to rail against my culture. I fear no betrayal on my part because, unlike Chicanas and other women of color who grew up white or who have only recently returned to their native cultural roots, I was totally immersed in mine. It wasn't until I went to high school that I "saw" whites. Until I worked on my master's degree I had not gotten within an arm's distance of them. I was totally immersed *en lo mexicano,* a rural, peasant, isolated, *mexicanismo.* To separate from my culture (as from my family) I had to feel competent enough on the outside and secure enough inside to live life on my own. Yet in leaving home I did not lose touch with my origins because *lo mexicano* is in my system. I am a turtle, wherever I go I carry "home" on my back. (LF 21)

This passage alludes to one of the major differences between these two writers. Whereas Moraga confesses her life of white-skin privilege and the feeling that she "sold out" her people, Anzaldúa asserts that the Mexicano traditions that systematically subordinate women have in fact sold *her* out. Rather than fearing the kind of cultural rejection Moraga so effectively describes throughout *Loving in the War Years,* Anzaldúa asserts that "if going home is denied me then I will have to stand and claim my space, making a new culture — *una cultura mestiza* — with my own lumber, my own bricks and mortar and my own feminist architecture" (LF 22). Contrasting her experience with that of women like Moraga, she maintains that the color of her skin contributed to her betrayal. "The dark-skinned woman has been silenced, gagged, caged, bound into servitude with marriage, bludgeoned for 300 years, sterilized and castrated in the twentieth century" (LF 22).

But Moraga too has been gagged. The dialogue between these lesbian cultural critics extends beyond the pages of their personal narratives, for they have produced texts that represent perspectives in the ongoing debate over Western and indigenous modes of perception. In one of the final journal entries in Moraga's autobiography she writes:

> Quiero decir that I know on the surface of things, this is not to make any sense. I spoke English at home. On the surface of things I am not supposed to feel that my language has been stripped from me — I am "born American." College English educated, but what I must admit is that I have felt in my writing that the English was not cutting it. Entiendes? That there is something else, deep and behind my heart and I want to hold it hot and bold in the hands of my writing and it will not come out sounding like English. Te prometo. No es ingles. And I have to wonder, is it so that I have felt "too much," "too emotional," "too sensitive" because I was trying to translate my feelings into English cadences? (L 141)

This kind of alienation occurs when an individual feels compelled to constantly "translate" herself; it arises when a racialized individual, through socialization in the dominant U.S. ideology, "learns" to be self-conscious rather than self-assured and adaptable in terms of a culture or language that varies from the mainstream. Moraga inadvertently represents the irony of individuals who have internalized Western modes of perception yet are unable to translate what they feel; as a consequence they find themselves expressing their desire to embrace the lost tongue of their oppressed ancestors in the language and conceptual paradigms of their oppressors.

Anzaldúa's borderland experience has diffused this cultural predicament by cultivating a *mestiza* consciousness that enables her to reject the binary oppositions she views as the simplistic by-products of Western thought. "Presently this infant language, this bastard language, Chicano Spanish, is not approved by any society," she tells us in her preface. "But we Chicanos no longer feel that we need to beg entrance . . . to translate to Anglos, Mexicans, and Latinos" (LF preface). Rather than concern herself with translation and the limitations of the English language, she focuses on the hybridity and the new modes of expression *mestizaje* generates.

> The work of *mestiza* consciousness is to break down the subject-object duality which keeps her a prisoner and to show in the flesh and through images in her work how duality is transcended. The answer to the problem between the white race and the colored, between males and females, lies in healing the split that originates in the very foundation of our lives, our culture, our languages and our thoughts. A massive uprooting of dualistic thinking in the individual and collective consciousness is the beginning of a long struggle, but one that could, in our best hopes, bring us to the end of rape, of violence, of war. (LF 80)

Ultimately Anzaldúa's discussion enables us to see how Moraga's grounding in Anglo American culture has in many ways restricted the feminist/cultural analysis in *Loving in the War Years* to an interrogation of the differences and interconnections between white women and women of color. Critical of "subject-object" dualities, Anzaldúa tries to uproot and resolve Moraga's theoretical quandary by incorporating a discussion of hybridity, "Mother Earth," and the legacy of her native ancestors.[19]

Explicating this familiar "feminist/nativist" resolution, Norma Alarcón suggest that

> for many writers the point is not so much to recover a lost "utopia" nor the "true" essence of our being, although, of course, there are those who long for the "lost origins," as well as those who feel a profound spiritual kinship with the "lost" — a spirituality whose resistant political implications must not be underestimated, but refocused for feminist change.[20]

Alarcón's provocative insights allow us to unpack Anzaldúa's controversial agenda, which seems on the surface to advocate restrictive nationalist resolutions. What we need to consider here is not so much what Anzaldúa proposes, but why she proposes it. More specifically, before we can refocus her text for "feminist change" we must come to terms with its motivating factors.[21]

"Entering into the Serpent" represents Anzaldúa's symbolic return to the native spirituality of another world, the land of the plumed serpent Quetzalcoatl — ancient Mexico. At times difficult to follow, the writing in this portion of the text is marked by the author's instinctive and emotional metaphysical explorations, which defy the logic of this world. The disjointed poetic prose in the next chapter, "*La herencia de Coatlicue*: The Coatlicue State" signals a dramatic shift in style and seems to suggest that Anzaldúa is experimenting with the language and philosophy of two worlds to make contact with her "lost origins." Anzaldúa's "Entering into the Serpent" prepares readers for a new-age discussion of ancient thought and belief by grounding it in the familiar, the religious ideology predominant in Mexico today. The chapter underscores hybridity by weaving an analysis of Mexican "folk" catholicism and pre-Columbian religious practices that emerges from her rendition of the story of la Virgen de Guadalupe and the Indian, Juan Diego.

> Today, *la Virgen de Guadalupe* is the single most potent religious, political and cultural image of the Chicano/ *mexicano*. She, like my race is a synthesis of the old world and the new, of the religion and culture of the two races in our psyche, the conquerors and the conquered. She is the symbol of the *mestizo* true to his or her Indian values. (LF 30)

Her comparison exposes an essentialist "womanist" agenda that seeks to transform modern patriarchal perceptions by subverting masculinist interpretations of religious mythology. This rhetorical method, linking ancient and new worlds, leads to a natural reflection on a number of indigenous deities that culminates with the Aztec goddess Coatlicue,

> one of the powerful images, or "archetypes," that inhabits, or passes through, my psyche. For me, *la Coatlicue* is the consuming internal whirlwind, the symbol of the underground aspects of the psyche. *Coatlicue* is the mountain,

the Earth Mother who conceived all celestial beings out of
her cavernous womb. Goddess of birth and death, *Coatlicue* gives and takes away life; she is the incarnation of
cosmic processes . . . she represents: duality in life, a synthesis of duality, and a third perspective — something more
than mere duality or a synthesis of duality. (LF 46)

Unlike the rhetoric of Chicano nationalism, Anzaldúa's brand
of new-age feminist nationalism privileges Coatlicue over her son,
the Aztec war-god Huitzilopochtli.[22] The emphasis on the earth-
goddess Coatlicue reconceptualizes cultural nationalism so that it
will inspire women (as opposed to men) to recognize their personal
power. For, like Paula Gunn Allen, Anzaldúa believes that "failure
to know your mother, that is your position and its attendant traditions, history, and place in the scheme of things, is failure to remember your significance, your reality, your right relationship to
earth and society."[23]

Although the perspective represented in this chapter raises political concerns about how viable or productive are the ideological
reversals Anzaldúa seems to propose, it illustrates the author's desire to define a creative space for Chicana inquiry. This new space
she identifies as the borderlands, a terrain that by its very nature
will sanction the integration of ancient and modern cultural beliefs
and encourage an active interrogation of the reliability of "traditional" interpretations of myth and history. For as Anzaldúa suggests to her female audience:

Culture forms our beliefs. We perceive the version of reality that it communicates. Dominant paradigms, prede-
fined concepts that exist as unquestionable, unchallenge-

able, are transmitted to us through the culture. Culture is made by those in power — men. Males make the rules and laws: women transmit them. (LF 16)

La Frontera's reconstruction of ancient religion, with its particular emphasis on women, articulates an oppositional system of beliefs aimed at subverting those in power. The text thus represents the author's attempt to animate women with a positive sense of self by returning to the indigenous homeland and recovering a lost tradition that valued and honored femaleness.

The text can, in fact, be thought of as a cultural exhibition that meticulously presents a variety of issues and influences that augment Chicana/Mexicana *mestiza* subjectivity.

My "stories" are acts encapsulated in time, "enacted" every time they are spoken aloud or read silently. I like to think of them as performances and not as inert and "dead" objects (as the aesthetics of Western culture think of art works). Instead, the work has an identity; it is a "who" or a "what" and contains the presences of persons, that is, incarnations of gods or ancestors or natural and cosmic powers. The work manifests the same needs as a person, it needs to be "fed," *la tengo que bañar y vestir.* (LF 67)

Clearly, Anzaldúa intends to resuscitate *mestizas* by revitalizing their abused cultural spirit. *La Frontera* thus functions as a cultural performance that conveys the author's challenge to conventional Anglo American modes of perception that tend to separate feeling from thinking.

Overall, the text's narrative design blurs the lines between history and myth, poetry and prose; as a consequence Anzaldúa vigorously interrogates the relationship between reality and fiction. Consequently *La Frontera* can be read as a complex intellectual project that challenges traditional interpretations of culture and history that have systematically subordinated and oppressed women. The first half of the book exhibits a variety of languages that in many instances remain intentionally untranslated; this symbolic act of cultural defiance may evoke anger, frustration, or confusion among readers denied complete understanding and invited to search for meaning in a way that corresponds to the daily experiences of the non-native speaker of English. Rather than allowing readers to simply engage in an intellectual analysis of her subject, Anzaldúa forces them to experience alienation and the pain of exclusion.

Like Moraga's autobiography, Anzaldúa's is as experimental as it is experiential. She improvises with form and language to facilitate the kind of cultural exchange and awareness that can only occur through reflexive analysis or firsthand experience. Excluded from significant portions of the textual dialogue, thrust into a foreign experience that privileges ancient indigenous practices over standards espoused by Western civilization, readers must confront the limitations of Eurocentric conceptions.

The final prose chapter, "*La conciencia de la mestiza/*Towards a New Consciousness," prepares readers for the poetry portion of the text, which, in Cherríe Moraga's assessment, enables Anzaldúa to represent the "real" material conditions that constitute borderland existence: "In some of the poetry — which is more narrative than lyrical — the mestiza/o reality takes on flesh."[24] The writing in this chapter balances poetic and essay forms in a style similar to Moraga's, which openly concedes a cultural ambiguity that stems from a variety of cultural influences. Here Anzaldúa's and Moraga's concerns come together, as the text points to the polymorphous subject identities encompassed by the Chicana classification:

> The new *mestiza* copes by developing a tolerance for contradictions, a tolerance for ambiguity. She learns to be an Indian in Mexican culture, to be Mexican from an Anglo point of view. She learns to juggle cultures. She has a plural personality, she operates in a pluralistic mode — nothing is thrust out, the good the bad and the ugly, nothing rejected, nothing abandoned. Not only does she sustain contradictions, she turns the ambivalence into something else. (LF 79)

Bridging Love, War, and the Borderlands

The quote with which I opened this chapter reflects upon the motivating factors that set the *Bridge* anthology in motion. Contrary to the writers' intent, it conveys much more than their subjective responses to oppression, effectively describing the way their text as a whole transformed feminist discourse. More specifically, in *Bridge* Moraga and Anzaldúa provide a blueprint for self-development: an initial recognition of the problem followed by a pragmatic design for social change. The model these authors describe, based on a dialectical paradigm, responds to challenge with counterchallenge. When writers use their craft to voice their challenge, this dialectical process takes on new dimensions, and "mere words on a page [begin] to transform themselves into a living entity."

Together Cherríe Moraga and Gloria Anzaldúa have produced a series of important texts that represent their firm commitment to women of color and feminist practices as well as their dedication to opening rather than closing feminist/culturalist agendas. When we consider the impact of *Bridge,* we understand that two Chicana coeditors, ahead of their time, organized a coalition of "women writers of color" that collectively initiated an important discussion about the politics of "difference."

This Bridge Called My Back set the agenda, articulating the concerns of women who had been systematically relegated to the margins of discourse, while *Loving in the War Years* and *Borderlands/La Frontera* refined it and carried it further. The Moraga/Anzaldúa trilogy resonates with multiplicity. The texts provide readers with a variety of Chicana motifs that enable others to consider difference and how it pertains to issues of regionality, sexuality, class, and gender. The issues they raise concerning language, culture, voice, and literary convention emerge consistently in all genres of Chicana writing.

Anzaldúa concludes her experimental autobiography with a series of poems that directly address hybridity and multiple subjectivity. "To Live in the Borderlands Means You," which brilliantly deconstructs essentialist notions, underscores the overall narrative intent of the three texts I have discussed in this chapter.

> To live in the Borderlands means you
>> are neither *hispana india negra espanola*
>> *ni gabacha, eres mestiza, mulata,* half breed
>> caught in the crossfire between camps
>> while carrying all five races on your back
>> not knowing which side to turn to, run from;

To live in the Borderlands means knowing
    that the *india* in you, betrayed for 500 years,
    is no longer speaking to you,
    that *mexicanas* call you *rajetas,*
    that denying the Anglo inside you
    is bad as having denied the Indian or Black;
Cuando vives en la frontera
    people walk through you, the wind steals your voice,
    you're a *burra, buey,* scapegoat,
    forerunner of a new race,
    half and half — both woman and man, neither —
    a new gender;
To live in the Borderlands mean to
    put *chile* in the borscht,
    eat whole wheat *tortillas,*
    speak Tex-Mex with a Brooklyn accent;
    be stopped by *la migra* at the border checkpoints;
Living in the Borderlands means you fight hard to
    resist the gold elixer beckoning from the bottle,
    the pull of the gun barrel,
    the rope crushing the hollow of your throat;
In the Borderlands
    you are the battleground
    where enemies are kin to each other;
    you are at home, a stranger,
    the border disputes have been settled
    the volley of shots have shattered the truce
    you are wounded, lost in action
    dead, fighting back;
To live in the Borderlands means

the mill with the razor white teeth wants to shred off
your olive-red skin, crush out the kernel, your heart
pound you pinch you roll you out
smelling like white bread but dead;
To survive the Borderlands
you must live *sin fronteras*
be a crossroads. (LF 194)

Notes

Introduction

1. Pat Mora, "Legal Alien," in *Chants* (Houston: Arte Publico, 1984), 52.
2. Stephen Greenblatt, *Renaissance Self-Fashioning: From More to Shakespeare* (Chicago: University of Chicago Press, 1980): 9.
3. The phrase "thick description" comes from Clifford Geertz, "Thick Description: Toward an Interpretive Theory of Culture," in *Interpretation of Cultures* (New York: Basic, 1973): 3–30.
4. Mario Suarez, "El Hoyo," in *Voices of Aztlan: Chicano Literature of Today,* ed. Dorothy Harth and Lewis Baldwin (New York: Mentor, 1974), 15.
5. See Terry Eagleton's "Rise of English" in *Literary Theory: An Introduction* (Minneapolis: University of Minnesota Press, 1983).

Chapter I

1. Fredric Jameson, *The Political Unconscious: Narrative as a Socially Symbolic Act* (Ithaca: Cornell University Press, 1981).

2. Because Mexican culture is a hybrid created by the Spanish intrusion, Paulo Freire's discourse on the effects of colonization on the consciousness of persons occupying an invaded territory adequately describes how the violence of the conquest culminated in the loss of identity for the people of Mexico. In cultural invasion the invaders are the subjects; those they invade are the objects in the process. "The invaders act; those they invade have only the illusion of acting, through the action of the invaders." Freire shows how cultural invasion creates mental ambiguity in the colonized, an estrangement from the self that leaves the colonized feeling inauthentic, impure, or incomplete. They appear to suffer from a deep inner duality, a realization that they combine oppressor and oppressed — they have internalized the colonizer's values by maintaining the colonialist structure that insures their own subordinate status. See Paulo Freire, *Pedagogy of the Oppressed,* trans. Myra Bergman Ramos (New York: Continuum, 1984).

3. The term *indigenous,* rather than identifying a romantic or nostalgic notion of an "authentic primitive," here alludes to a cultural configuration that results from a specific historical dynamic — the Conquest.

4. The conquest of Mexico generated a confusion that caused the natives to lose their sense of a social self. This national bewilderment, characterized by feelings of inauthenticity, fear, and alienation, served as a catalyst for a series of discussions concerning Mexican identity. With the rise of the mestizo in the twentieth century came the vigorous philosophical debate on the question of *Mexicanidad.* With Samuel Ramos and José Vasconcelos came a push to consider the conflicts that stemmed from the blending of European and Indian cultures. Thus Mexican self-fashioning became a focus that contributed to the concept of *mestizaje* or, in today's terms, *hybridization.* I am grateful to Jesus Contreras for contributing to my understanding of Mexican philosophy.

5. Rosa Linda Fregoso, "Born in East L.A. and the Politics of Representation," *Cultural Studies* 4, 3 (1990): 268.

6. Gloria Anzaldúa, *Borderlands/La Frontera: The New Mestiza* (San Francisco: Spinsters/Aunt Lute, 1987).

7. Barbara Harlow, *Resistance Literature* (New York: Metheun, 1987), 28. Julia Kristeva, *The Kristeva Reader* (New York: Columbia University Press, 1986).

8. Chela Sandoval's "U.S. Third World Feminism: The Theory and the Method of Oppositional Consciousness in the Postmodern World" describes in detail the philosophical issues involved in Chicana social resistance. *Genders,* no. 10 (Spring 1991): 1–25.

9. Sylvia Harvey, *May '68 and Film Culture* (London: British Film Institute, 1978), 100–101.

10. Jane H. Bayes, *Minority Politics and Ideologies in the United States* (Novato, Calif.: Chandler and Sharp, 1982), 66–67.

11. My use of the hyphen here reflects the practice during this time period. Only after a series of debates and political struggles was the hyphen dropped; although grammatically correct, its use signified individuals who occupied a subordinate social position and who were viewed as less than "all American."

12. Starhawk, "Consciousness, Politics, & Magic," in *The Politics of Women's Spirituality: Essays on the Rise of Spiritual Power within the Feminist Movement,* ed. Charlene Spretnak (New York: Anchor, 1982), 181.

13. Simone de Beauvoir comments on the kind of attitude that contributes to this suppression: " 'Man can think of himself without woman. She cannot think of herself without man.' And she is simply what man decrees; thus she is called 'the sex,' by which is meant that she appears essentially to the male as a sexual being. For him she is sex — absolute sex, no less. She is defined and differentiated with reference to man and not he with reference to her; she is the incidental, the inessential as opposed to the essential. He is the Subject, he is the Absolute — she is the Other." *The Second Sex,* trans. and ed. H. M. Pashley (New York: Vintage, 1974), xix.

14. Although Ramón Saldívar's brilliant notion of "the dialectics of difference" was developed as narrative strategy for demystifying the relations between minority and dominant cultures, I am employing it here to signify difference and struggle between minority cultures. See Ramón Saldívar, *Chicano Narrative: The Dialectics of Difference* (Madison: University of Wisconsin Press, 1990).

15. Denise Segura points out that many Chicanas are confronted with triple oppression: "Although class and race bestow and/or limit access to political and economic power, women within each class category and racial/ethnic group are subordinate relative to men. . . . The per-

vasiveness of gender inequality transcends class and points to the necessity of incorporating gender into social analyses of women, including Chicanas." Segura suggests that we must take into account the relationship between gender and race/class oppression if we are to construct a social theory that reasons with Chicana experience(s). The cumulative effects of triple oppression place women of color in a subordinate social and economic position relative to both men and the entire dominant Anglo American population. Segura's approach, representative of an emergent mode of sociological analysis, attempts to reckon with this male/female, Chicana/mainstream feminist hiatus. Denise Segura, "Chicanas and Triple Oppression in the Labor Force," in *Chicana Voices: Intersections of Race, Class, and Gender,* ed. Ricardo Romo (Austin: Center for Mexican American Studies, 1986), 48.

16. M. M. Bakhtin, *The Dialogic Imagination: Four Essays,* ed. Michael Holquist (Austin: University of Texas Press, 1981), 146.

17 Gloria Anzaldúa, "La Prieta," in *This Bridge Called My Back: Writings by Radical Women of Color,* ed. Cherríe Moraga and Gloria Anzaldúa (Watertown, Mass.: Persephone, 1981), 209.

18 Marta Ester Sánchez, *Contemporary Chicana Poetry* (Berkeley: University of California Press, 1985), 7.

19 Cordelia Candelaria, *Chicano Poetry* (Westport, Conn.: Greenwood, 1986), 66. Subsequent citations of this work are noted by page number in parentheses in the text.

20. My decision to cite Candelaria's text in this chapter stems from her choice (unlike Juan Bruce-Novoa's in *Chicano Poetry,* which limits its analysis of Chicana contributions to a chapter on Bernice Zamora without raising the gender question) to discuss a variety of Chicana writers who seek to balance their concern for poetic style with their Chicana feminist agendas. See Juan Bruce-Novoa, *Chicano Poetry: A Response to Chaos* (Austin: University of Texas Press, 1982).

21. Linda Gordon, "What's New in Women's History," in *Feminist Studies/Critical Studies,* ed. Teresa de Lauretis (Bloomington: Indiana University Press, 1986), 30.

22. Raymond Williams, *Marxism and Literature* (New York: Oxford University Press, 1977).

23. Saldívar, *Chicano Narrative,* 173.

24. Harvey, *May '68 and Film Culture,* 72.

25. bell hooks, *Talking Back* (Boston: South End, 1984), 8.
26. Saldívar, *Chicano Narrative,* 173.

Chapter 2

1. The white assumption to which I refer considers racial/cultural differences among women in black/white terms only, implying that "black" represents the universal signifier of difference. Interestingly, the feminist emphasis on blackness as universal "other" has not appeased Alice Walker, who discursively distances herself and other African American women with the term *womanist* to signify African American feminism. Additionally, a number of women of color have challenged the feminist approaches that fail to move beyond black/white racial binaries: See for example Cherríe Moraga and Gloria Anzaldúa, eds., *This Bridge Called My Back: Writings by Radical Women of Color* (Watertown, Mass.: Persephone, 1981); Gloria Anzaldúa, *Hacienda Caras: Making Face, Making Soul* (San Francisco: Aunt Lute Foundation, 1990); Sonia Saldívar-Hull, "Feminism on the Border: From Gender Politics to Geopolitics," in *Criticism in the Borderlands: Studies in Chicano Literature, Culture, and Ideology,* ed. Héctor Calderón and José David Saldívar (Durham, N.C.: Duke University Press, 1991), 203–20.
2. Marilyn Strathern, "Dislodging a World View: Challenge and Counter-Challenge in the Relation between Feminism and Anthropology." Lecture at the Research Center for Women's Studies, University of Adelaide, Adelaide, Australia, 4 July 1984.
3. I have borrowed the phrase "suppressed text" from Fredric Jameson, *The Political Unconscious: Narrative As a Socially Symbolic Act* (Ithaca: Cornell University Press, 1981), 10.
4. I can still remember the shock I felt when I discovered in Sociology 100 that I was a "marginal person." The discipline of anthropology has also coined a term for individuals operating within two cultural systems — *cultural broker.*
5. Here I am alluding to Terry Eagleton's ideas regarding silences in the text that reveal not only the presence of ideology but also the relationship of specific writers to the modes of production.

6. Alvina Quintana, "Language, Power, & Women: A Hermeneutic Interpretation," *Critical Perspectives: Women, Race, & Class in a Cultural Context* 2, 1 (Fall 1984): 10–20.

7. Adrienne Rich, "When We Dead Awaken: Writing as Revision," in *On Lies, Secrets, and Silence: Selected Prose, 1966–1978* (New York: Norton, 1979), 18.

8. Alison Jaggar, *Feminist Politics and Human Nature* (Brighton, Eng.: Harvester, 1983), 11.

9. Susan Krieger, *The Mirror Dance* (Philadelphia: Temple University Press, 1983), 196.

10. Terry Eagleton, *Marxism and Literary Criticism* (Berkeley: University of California Press, 1976), 18. Clifford Geertz, *The Interpretation of Cultures* (New York: Basic, 1973), 3–30.

11. See Nancy Hartsock, *Money, Sex, and Power* (Baltimore: Johns Hopkins University Press, 1983).

12. Here I am alluding to Marxist theory in general and Fredric Jameson's Marxist criticism in particular as they relate to the fashioning of identity in terms of the historical moment. That the women's movement was reactivated in the 1960s, for instance, is of particular relevance to the types of questions women began asking about gender differences.

13. Although a number of other musical forms are based upon call and response, I found myself drawn to the classical fugue, which I became acquainted with in a graduate seminar on women in the blues taught by Angela Davis. My selection reflects my preference, just as it does my socialization and education in the United States. For a detailed analysis of the meaning of music see Sidney Finkelstein, *How Music Expresses Ideas* (New York: International, 1970).

14. Hayden White's *Metahistory: The Historical Imagination in Nineteenth-Century Europe* (Baltimore: Johns Hopkins University Press, 1973) has been especially helpful in developing my modes of poetic discourse. His discussion of Kenneth Burke's "master trope" irony has become particularly relevant to my "new-vision" stage in Chicana literature.

15. Helene Cixous, "The Laugh of the Medusa," in *New French Feminisms,* ed. Elaine Marks and Isabelle de Courtivron (Boston: University of Massachusetts Press, 1980).

16. Annette Kuhn, *Women's Pictures* (London: Routledge and Kegan Paul, 1982), 13–18.

17. Tomas Ybarra, paper presented at the National Association for Chicano Studies, 1986. William C. Dowling, *Jameson, Althusser, Marx: An Introduction to the Political Unconscious* (Ithaca: Cornell University Press, 1984), 21.

18. Lorna Dee Cervantes, *Emplumada* (Pittsburgh: University of Pittsburgh Press, 1981), 41.

19. See Norma Alarcón's discussion of the bicultural experience of Chicanas in "What Kind of Lover Have You Made Me, Mother? Towards a Theory of Chicanas' Feminism and Cultural Identity through Poetry," in *Women of Color: Perspectives on Feminism and Identity,* ed. Audrey T. McKloskey, Occasional Papers Series, vol. 1, no. 1 (Bloomington: Indiana University Womens' Studies, 1985), 85–110.

20. Lucha Corpi, "Marina Virgin," in *Fireflight: Three Latin American Poets,* ed. and trans. Catherine Rodriguez-Nieto (Berkeley: Oyez, 1976), 79.

21. Jagger, *Feminist Politics and Human Nature.*

22. Lorna Dee Cervantes, "You Cramp My Style, Baby," *El Fuego de Aztlan* 1, 4 (Summer 1977): 39.

23. Cherríe Moraga, *Loving in the War Years* (Boston: South End, 1983), 99.

24. Eagleton, *Marxism and Literary Criticism,* 23.

25. Gina Valdes, *There Are No Madmen Here* (San Diego: Maize, 1982), 48, 32.

26. Gina Valdes, *Comiendo Lumbre* (Colorado Springs: Maize, 1986), 58.

27. Juan Felipe Herrera, "The Califas Movimiento," *Poetry Flash,* March 1984.

28. Moraga, *Loving in the War Years,* 62–63.

29. Paulo Freire, *Pedagogy of the Oppressed,* trans. Myra Bergman Ramos (New York: Continuum, 1984), 33.

30. Sandra Cisneros, "Born Bad," in *The House on Mango Street* (Houston: Arte Publico, 1984), 56.

31. Teresa de Lauretis, *Alice Doesn't* (Bloomington: Indiana University Press, 1982), 36.

32. Lydia Camarillo, "Mi Reflejo," in *La Palabra* (Tucson: Post Litho, 1980), 73.

Chapter 3

1. Fredric Jameson, *The Geopolitical Aesthetic: Cinema and Space in the World System* (Bloomington: Indiana University Press), 1992, 9–10.

2. See Juan Bruce-Novoa's in-depth examination of the place of Chicano literature within the traditional literary arena, "The Space of Chicano Literature," *De Colores* 1, 4 (1975): 22–42. For a thorough discussion of Silvia Bovenschen's notion of feminist aesthetics, see "Is There a Feminine Aesthetic?" in *Feminist Aesthetics,* ed. Gisela Ecker, trans. Harriet Anderson (Boston: Beacon, 1985), 23–50. I am also alluding to Hal Foster's definition of the "anti-aesthetic"; see "Postmodernism: A Preface," in *The Anti-Aesthetic: Essays on Postmodern Culture* (Port Townsend, Wash.: Bay, 1983).

3. For a survey of nine critical reviews on *Mango Street* see Pedro Gutierrez-Revuelta's essay "Genero e ideologia en el libro de Sandra Cisneros: *The House on Mango Street,*" in *Critica: A Journal of Critical Essays* 1, 3 (Fall 1986): 48–59.

4. Terry Eagleton, *Literary Theory: An Introduction* (Minneapolis: University of Minnesota Press, 1983), 201.

5. Even though Mikhail Bakhtin has argued that the novel form defies finalization, his emphasis on prosaics leaves me questioning whether Cisneros's clearly poetic work constitutes a novel. It seems to surpass Bakhtin's categories, as it blurs many genres.

6. Sandra Cisneros, "Do You Know Me? I Wrote *The House on Mango Street,*" *Americas Review* 15, 1 (Spring 1987): 79.

7. Sandra Cisneros, *The House on Mango Street* (Houston: Arte Publico, 1984), 5. Subsequent citations of this work are noted by page number in parentheses in the text, as: (M 81).

8. Rosaura Sánchez, "Ethnicity, Ideology, and Academia," in *Americas Review* 15, 1 (Spring 1987): 81.

9. Even though Cisneros is developing a social critique, it is one that has gone unnoticed by some Chicano critics. In a review of *Mango Street* in the *Austin Chronicle,* 10 August 1984, Juan Rodriguez comments: "That Esperanza chooses to leave Mango St., chooses to move away from her social/cultural base to become more 'Anglicized,' more individualistic; that she chooses to move from the real to the fantasy plane of the world as the only means of accepting and surviving the limited

and limiting social conditions of her barrio becomes problematic to the more serious reader."

10. Susan Lanser, *The Narrative Act: Point of View in Prose Fiction* (Princeton: Princeton University Press, 1981), 117–18.

11. See Tey Diana Rebolledo, "Abuelitas: Mythology and Integration in Chicana Literature," in *Woman of Her Word: Hispanic Women Write,* ed. Evagelina Vigil (Houston: Arte Publico, 1983), 148–58.

12. According to Malcolm X, members of the Nation of Islam in the United States used the "X" to symbolize the true African name that they could never know. The use of "X" in this way — to liberate African Americans, is analogous with Esperanza's proposed use of Zeze the X.

13. James Clifford, "On Ethnographic Allegory," in *Writing Culture: The Poetics and Politics of Ethnography,* ed. James Clifford and George E. Marcus (Berkeley: University of California Press, 1986), 98.

14. Adrienne Rich, "When We Dead Awaken: Writing as Revision," in *On Lies, Secrets, and Silence: Selected Prose, 1966–1978* (New York: Norton, 1979), 35.

15. Clifford, "On Ethnographic Allegory," 100. For a thorough discussion of internal oppression, see Paulo Freire, *Pedagogy of the Oppressed* (New York: Continuum, 1984).

16. Freire, *Pedagogy of the Oppressed,* 151.

17. Franz Fanon, *The Wretched of the Earth,* trans. Constance Farrington (New York: Grove, 1966).

18. *Mango,* a Ceylanese word, is in common use among English speakers, a practice that illustrates my point.

19. Sandra Cisneros, "Ghosts and Voices," *Americas Review* 15, 1 (Spring 1987): 72–73.

20. Bettina Aptheker, *Tapestries of Life: Women's Work, Consciousness, and the Meaning of Daily Experience* (Amherst: University of Massachusetts Press, 1989), 39.

21. In Greimasian terms the traditional modes of female existence evolve out of four sets of contradictions created by the primary contradiction that women in patriarchal systems are confronted with — the conflict between married and single status. The semiotic rectangle represents the nucleus of an ideological system that contains the four terms for female existence, illustrating Cisneros's narrative possibilities.

Recalling Fredric Jameson's application of Greimas in chapter 5 of *The Political Unconscious* allows us to understand that "the place of characters and of a character system is opened up only at the point at which the mind seeks further release from its ideological closure by projecting combinations of these various schemes: to work through the various possible combinations is then concretely to imagine the life forms, or the characterological types, that can embody and manifest such contradictions, which otherwise remain abstract and repressed." *The Political Unconscious: Narrative As a Socially Symbolic Act* (Ithaca: Cornell University Press, 1981), 254.

22. Fanon, *The Wretched of the Earth,* 190.
23. Rich, "When We Dead Awaken," 37.

Chapter 4

1. On a basic level this point can be illustrated by reflecting on the way terms like *feminist* and *Chicana* modify our understanding and expectations of literature and anthropology, transforming conservative thinking by creating the opportunity for alternative or more inclusive types of analysis.
2. George E. Marcus and Michael M. J. Fischer, *Anthropology as Cultural Critique: An Experimental Moment in the Human Sciences* (Chicago: University of Chicago Press, 1986), 18.
3. Marjorie Shostak, *Nisa: The Life and Words of a Kung Woman* (New York: Vintage, 1981), 21. Subsequent citations of this work are noted by page number in parentheses in the text, as: (Nisa 40).
4. Hayden White, *On Narrative,* ed. W.J.T. Mitchell (Chicago: University of Chicago Press, 1980), 23.
5. Ibid., 13.
6. Ana Castillo, *The Mixquiahuala Letters* (Binghamton, N.Y.: Bilingual Press/Editorial Bilingue, 1986).
7. Clifford Geertz, *The Interpretation of Cultures* (New York: Basic, 1973); Castillo, *The Mixquiahuala Letters,* 46.

8. Steven Greenblatt, *Renaissance Self-Fashioning: From More to Shake-speare* (Chicago: University of Chicago Press, 1980), 9.

9. Norma Alarcón, "What Kind of Lover Have You Made Me, Mother? Towards a Theory of Chicanas' Feminism and Cultural Identity through Poetry," in *Women in Color: Perspectives on Feminism and Identity,* ed. Audrey T. McKloskey, Occasional Papers Series, vol. 1, no. 1 (Bloomington: Indiana University Women's Studies Program, 1985), 85–110.

10. James Clifford, "On Ethnographic Allegory," in *Writing Culture: The Poetics and Politics of Ethnography,* ed. James Clifford and George E. Marcus (Berkeley: University of California Press, 1986), 109.

11. Linda Hutcheon, *A Theory of Parody: The Teachings of Twentieth-Century Art Forms* (New York: Methuen, 1985), 53.

12. Eric R. Wolf, *Europe and the People without History* (Berkeley: University of California Press, 1982), 13.

13. Umberto Eco, *The Role of the Reader: Explorations in the Semiotics of Texts* (Bloomington: Indiana University Press, 1979), 63.

14. Marilyn Strathern, "Dislodging a World View: Challenge and Counter-Challenge in the Relationship between Feminism and Anthropology." Lecture at the Research Center for Women's Studies, University of Adelaide, Adelaide, Australia, 4 July 1984.

Chapter 5

1. Kathryn Rios, " 'And You Know What I Have to Say Isn't Always Pleasant': Translating the Unspoken Word in Cisneros' *Woman Hollering Creek,*" in *Chicana (W)Rites,* ed. Maria Herrera-Sobek and Helena Maria Viramontes (Berkeley: Third Woman, forthcoming).

2. Although many Chicano writers acknowledge the overall importance of folk culture and the corrido oral tradition, few have explored the ways they affect women's literary practices. For extended treatments of the corrido tradition see José Limón, *Mexican Ballads, Chicano Poems: History and Influence in Mexican-American Poetry* (Berkeley: University of California Press, 1992), and Ramón Saldívar, *Chicano Narrative: The Dialectics of Difference* (Madison: University of Wisconsin Press, 1990).

3. Yolanda Broyles, "Hinojosa's Klail City y sus alrededores: Oral Culture and Print Culture in *The Rolando Hinojosa Reader: Essays Historical and Critical,* ed. José David Saldívar (Houston: Arte Publico, 1985), 112.

4. Yolanda Broyles-Gonzáles, *Teatro Campesino: Four Cardinal Points* (Austin: University of Texas Press, 1994).

5. Yolanda J. Broyles, "Women in El Teatro Campesino: '?Apoco Estaba Molacha la Virgen de Guadalupe?' "in *Chicana Voices: Intersections of Class, Race, and Gender,* ed. Ricardo Romo (Austin: Center for Mexican American Studies, 1986), 164.

6. Ibid., 186.

7. The term *Chicano* has in the past been used to refer to both men and women. My use here also refers to both men and women, yet I also intend the term to call to mind the tension created by the male-centered space of Chicano literature as described in Juan Bruce-Novoa's essay, "The Space of Chicano Literature," *De Colores* 1, 4 (1975): 22–42.

8. See Hazel Carby, *Reconstructing Womanhood: The Emergence of the Afro-American Woman Novelist* (New York: Oxford University Press, 1987). Carby's discussion of the ideologies of womanhood has shown that womanhood is culturally, socially, and historically constructed. Chavez uses the phrase "spirit of womanhood" to suggest that a specific essence belongs to the category "woman." Although we understand that universal notions of womanhood do not exist, we must acknowledge the question that Chavez is grappling with as a feminist concern, an important issue that has preoccupied women's studies and gender studies programs around the globe.

9. Denise Chavez, "Novena Narrativas y Ofrendas Nuevomexicanas," *Americas Review,* 15, 3–4 (1987): 85. Subsequent citations of this work are noted by page number in parentheses in the text, as: (NN 16).

10. Vicki Ruiz sums up this social placement by suggesting that "in Chicano scholarship, Chicanas are invisible; and in women's studies, Chicanas are exotic — the 'other' of the 'other.' " For a thorough discussion of this problem, see the introduction to *Building with Our Hands: New Directions in Chicana Studies,* ed. Adela de la Torre and Beatriz M. Pesquera (Berkeley: University of California Press, 1993), 3.

11. Sandra Gilbert and Susan Gubar, *The Madwoman in the Attic: The Woman Writer of the Nineteenth-Century Literary Imagination* (New Haven: Yale University Press, 1979), 64.
12. Hazel Carby argues that dominant notions of domesticity and womanhood impacted the cultural productions of white and African American women writers of the period in distinct ways. Antithetical to Anglo American women's and African American men's cultural production, the African American "literary woman" was placed in a social position that challenged all the prevailing conceptions of womanhood. Carby, *Reconstructing Womanhood.*
13. Angie Chabram-Dernersesian argues that a variety of modes of representation are available to Chicana subjectivity; the term Chicana itself signifies "a field for multiple cultural critiques (inside and outside the Chicano community) that unsettle previously conferred identities: Anglo, Hispanic, Pocho, Mexican American, Spanish, and Chicano." The multiple cultural critiques Chabram-Dernersesian outlines undoubtedly influence what some critics identify as a Chicana ambivalence. See Angie Chabram-Dernersesian, "And, Yes . . . the Earth Did Part: On the Splitting of Chicana/o Subjectivity," in *Building with Our Hands,* ed. de la Torre and Pesquera, 38.
14. John Bradshaw's work on family systems has provided me with a useful approach for understanding how family and cultural systems influence personal-identity formation. By modifying his theory we can illustrate how cultural systems also affect ethnic- and gender-identity formation. See John Bradshaw, *On the Family: A Revolutionary Way of Self-Discovery* (Deerfield Beach, Fla.: Health Communications, 1988).
15. For a detailed explanation of the meaning of yoga see Lucy Lidell, with Narayani and Giris Rabinovitch, *The Sivananda Companion to Yoga* (New York: Simon and Schuster, 1983), 15.
16. Victor Turner, *The Anthropology of Performance* (New York: Performing Arts Journal Publications, 1987).
17. Denise Chavez, *The Last of the Menu Girls* (Houston: Arte Publico, 1986), 13. Subsequent citations of this work are noted by page number in parentheses in the text, as: (MG 53).
18. Suzanne Juhasz suggests a method for considering the differences between male and female discourse: "When you ask a women, "what

happened?" you often get an answer in a style that [is] . . . circumstantial, complex, and contextual. You hear a series of "he saids" and "she saids;" you are told what they were wearing, where they were sitting, what they were eating; and slowly the story unrolls. The woman is omitting no detail that she can remember, because all details have to do with her sense of the nature of "what happened." A man, on the other hand, will characteristically summarize: give you the gist, the result, the *point* of the event. . . . In their form, women's lives tend to be like the stories that they tell: they show less a pattern of linear development towards some clear goal than one repetitive, cumulative, cyclical structure." Even though Juhasz's argument seems reductive in that it reflects an essentialist sensibility that attributes particular behavior to gender, the cyclical structure she suggests accurately describes Chavez's narrative style. Suzanne Juhasz, "Towards a Theory of Form in Feminist Autobiography: Kate Millett's *Flying and Sita*; Maxine Hong Kingston's *The Woman Warrior*," in *Women's Autobiography: Essays, and Criticism,* ed. Estelle C. Jelinek (Bloomington: Indiana University Press, 1980), 223–24.

19. For a more thorough discussion of this feminine-feminist tension, see Linda Gordon, "What's New in Women's History," in *Feminist Studies/Critical Studies,* ed. Teresa de Lauretis (Bloomington: Indiana University Press, 1986), 30.

20. Turner, *The Anthropology of Performance,* 76.

21. Barbara Harlow, *Resistance Literature* (New York: Methuen, 1987), 81.

Chapter 6

1. Cherríe Moraga and Gloria Anzaldúa, eds., *This Bridge Called My Back: Writings by Radical Women of Color* (Watertown, Mass.: Persephone, 1981), xxiii.

2. Norma Alarcón, "This Bridge Called My Back and Anglo-American Feminism," in *Criticism in the Borderlands: Studies in Chicano Literature, Culture, and Ideology,* ed. Héctor Calderón and José David Saldívar (Durham, N.C.: Duke University Press, 1991), 29.

3. Teresa de Lauretis, "The Technology of Gender," in *Technologies of*

Gender: Essays on Theory, Film, and Fiction (Bloomington: Indiana University Press, 1987), 10.

4. Moraga and Anzaldúa, *This Bridge,* xiii.

5. Ibid., xxiv.

6. Alarcón, "This Bridge Called My Back," 11.

7. Moraga and Anzaldúa, *This Bridge,* viii.

8. José Saldívar, *The Dialectics of Our America: Genealogy, Cultural Critique, and Literary History* (Durham, N.C.: Duke University Press, 1991), 143.

9. Tey Diana Rebolledo makes the argument that Chicana poets use the sign of the *abuelita* (grandmother) either to link grandparents with cultural heritage and the past or to suggest the importance of these "familial relationships to the writer." Moraga's reference seems to follow the trend, but, as reflected in the overall experimental form of her text, she takes the convention further. Her opening pages provide an analysis that in many ways parallels Rebolledo's poetic mode of discussion. See Tey Diana Rebolledo, "Abuelitas: Mythology and Integration in Chicana Literature," *Woman of Her Word: Hispanic Women Write,* ed. Evangelina Vigil (Houston: Arte Publico, 1983), 148–58.

10. Cherríe Moraga, *Loving in the War Years* (Boston: South End, 1983), iii. Subsequent citations of this work are noted by page number in parentheses in the text, as: (L 45). I have corrected the original text wherein Moraga spells *gabacho* (white man) as *gavacho.* This error, along with many others throughout the text, reflects the author's limited experience with the Spanish language. She has apparently grown up hearing the language of her mother but, at least until this point in her life, had limited formal education as well as little practice with reading and writing Spanish, a weakness she discusses in her final essay, "A Long Line of Vendidas."

11. See Norma Alarcón, "Interview with Cherríe Moraga," in *Third Woman,* vol. 3 (Bloomington, Ind.: Third Woman Press, 1986): 127–34.

12. It is primarily this chapter that has led Donna Haraway to conclude that "Moraga's writing, her superb literacy, is presented in her poetry as the same kind of violation as Malinche's mastery of the conqueror's language — a violation, an illegitimate production that allows sur-

vival." See Donna Haraway, *Simians, Cyborgs, and Women: The Re-invention of Nature* (New York: Routledge, 1991), 175.

13. Moraga and Anzaldúa, *This Bridge,* 198.

14. Gloria Anzaldúa, *Borderlands/La Frontera: The New Mestiza* (San Francisco: Spinsters/Aunt Lute Press, 1987): 21. Subsequent citations of this work are noted by page number in parentheses in the text, as: (LF 48).

15. I find interesting the way Anzaldúa's text resonates wtih Susan Griffin's *Woman and Nature* (New York: Harper and Row, 1978). Both narrative projects attempt to refine patriarchal attitudes toward women by articulating arguments that emphasize the basics. Each author elects to rewrite Western thought by representing matriarchal influences that begin with the female's relationship to the earth. Obviously this narrative strategy is aimed at building women's self-esteem by providing them with a positive female interpretation of life. In "Myth and Comparative Cultural Nationalism" Genaro Padilla reflects on the "close relationship between a people's desire to determine their own political fortunes and their passion to restore their own cultural mythos, a vital psychic component of national identity which gives energy and purpose to their political struggle." His analysis is useful for unpacking Anzaldúa's feminist project, which like the 1960s version of Chicano nationalism aims to restore a cultural mythos that will help mend what she views as the Chicana shattered psyche. In Fanonian terms, she is involved in a narrative project that seeks to restore or reinvent the native past. For a thorough discussion of the relationship between political upheaval and nativist artistic projects, see Padilla's essay in *Aztlan: Essays on the Chicano Homeland,* ed. Rudolfo A. Anaya and Francisco Lomeli (Albuquerque: Academia/El Norte Publications, 1989), 111–35.

16. Renato Rosaldo, *Culture and Truth: The Remaking of Social Analysis* (Boston: Beacon, 1989), 216.

17. Sonia Saldívar-Hull, "Feminism on the Border: From Gender Politics to Geopolitics," in *Criticism in the Borderlands: Studies in Chicano Literature, Culture, and Ideology,* ed. Héctor Calderón and José David Saldívar, (Durham, N.C.: Duke University Press, 1991), 213.

18. J. Saldívar, *The Dialectics of Our America,* 83.

19. Anzaldúa's emphasis on the native woman grounds her discussion of

some of the ancient goddesses of the Southwest. She builds an argument that corresponds with the work of new-age writer Vicki Nobel, who dedicates her latest book in words that seem to articulate Anzaldúa's intimate convictions — "to the Dark Goddess, who has been rejected and demonized by patriarchal culture and lies in women. Her awakening is the source of energy and healing power, for us as individuals and for the planet. This work is intentionally devoted to that cause. May She arise in us and bring peace on earth again." See Vicki Nobel, *Shakti Woman: Feeling Our Fire, Healing Our World — The New Female Shamanism* (San Francisco: HarperCollins, 1991).

20. Norma Alarcón, "Chicana Feminism: In the Tracks of 'the' Native Woman," *Cultural Studies* 4, 3 (October 1990): 251.

21. Anzaldúa seems to advocate a complex essentialist sensibility that attempts to reconstruct the philosophy of ancient Mexico in order to redefine women. This approach raises serious problems in that it recreates the difficulties and limitations prevalent in Chicano nationalism by simply reversing categories, attempting to recover Aztlan in female. Diana Fuss's argument regarding the deployment of essentialism is extremely useful in this context. Diana Fuss, *Essentially Speaking: Feminism, Nature, & Difference* (New York: Routledge, 1989).

22. Laurette Sejourne recounts the Aztec myth of Huitzilopochtli's conception, which strangely resembles that of Christ: "It is said that one day while she was sweeping a feathery ball descended upon her like a lump of thread, and she took it and put it in her bosom close to her belly, beneath her petticoats, and after having swept she wished to take hold of it and could not find it, from which they say she became pregnant." Laurette Sejourne, *Burning Water: Thought and Religion in Ancient Mexico* (London: Thames and Hudson, 1957), 159.

23. Paula Gunn Allen, "Who Is Your Mother? Red Roots of White Feminism," in *The Graywolf Annual Five: Multicultural Literacy,* ed. Rich Simonson and Scott Walker (St. Paul, Minn.: Graywolf), 13.

24. Cherríe Moraga, "Algo Secretamente Àmado," review of *Borderlands/La Frontera,* by Gloria Anzaldúa, in *Third Woman: The Sexuality of Latinas,* vol. 4, ed. Norma Alarcón, Ana Castillo, and Cherríe Moraga (Berkeley: Third Woman Press, 1989), 151–56.

Index

Index

Index

Index